COMMON BONDS

Anti-Bias Teaching
in a
Diverse Society

Deborah A. Byrnes and
Gary Kiger, Editors

Association for Childhood Education International
11501 Georgia Avenue, Suite 315, Wheaton, MD 20902
301-942-2443 • 800-423-3563

2nd Edition

Anne Watson Bauer, Director of Publications/Editor
Deborah Jordan Kravitz, Production Editor

Cover:
Drawing provided by Utah State Office
of Education, Migrant Education Program,
Robert Winkelkotter, artist
Photographs:
Page 6, 10, 64, © 1996 Robert Finken
Page 22 © 1994 Jonathan A. Meyers
Page 48 © 1996 Jim Whitmer
Page 106 © 1996 Cleo Freelance Photo

Library of Congress Cataloging-in-Publication Data
Common bonds : anti-bias teaching in a diverse society/Deborah A. Byrnes and Gary
    Kiger, editors, — 2nd ed.
        p.   cm.
    Includes bibliographical references.
    Contents: Addressing race, ethnicity, and culture in the classroom / Deborah A.
Byrnes — Living with our deepest differences / Charles C. Haynes — Ability
differences in the classroom / Mara Sapon-Shevin — Class differences / Ellen
Davidson and Nancy Schniedewind — Language diversity in the classroom /
Deborah A. Byrnes and Diana Cortez — Gender equity in the classroom / Beverly
Hardcastle Stanford— Integrating anti-bias education / James J. Barta — Diversity in
the classroom / Karen Matsumoto-Grah.
    ISBN 0-87173-137-1
    1. Multicultural education—United States.   I. Byrnes, Deborah A.   II. Kiger,
Gary.
LC1099.3.C64   1996
370.117'0973—dc21   96-39200
                                                                              CIP

Foreword

Geneva Gay

One of the most prevalent and salient features of humanity in general and American culture in particular is pluralism. It stems from many different sources—ideology, politics, religion, national origins, language, ethnicity, social class, gender, personal experiences and individual abilities. The general trend in the past has been for American institutions to acknowledge and celebrate those select dimensions of diversity in their official policies and actions that served economic and political ends, but aggressively to ignore and deny others. Schools served a major role in this latter function.

For the longest time, education in the United States was thought of as "the great equalizer." All students were to be treated the same, and thus homogenized into a common culture and class. The problem with this theory was twofold. First, it simply was not true that students from various social, cultural, racial, ethnic and linguistic backgrounds were treated with the same dignity and respect within the context of the educational process. Second, a single cultural standard of normalcy—that of the dominant group with its Eurocentric orientation—was imposed upon all students as *the* acceptable way of believing, feeling and behaving. In effect, the schools and other institutions worked in concert to practice cultural hegemony toward many of the diverse groups that make up society.

Despite these concerted efforts to make all individuals within society and schools conform to a middle-class, Anglocentric model, cultural pluralism prevailed. It is now resurfacing with renewed vigor and replenishing vitality. The United States and its schools are becoming even more diversified than they were in the past. Change is due to an increasing self-acceptance among culturally diverse groups, which demands that others respect their right to be different. A new era in immigration is bringing peoples from areas of the world and cultural backgrounds significantly different from previous immigration patterns, with greater growth rates among people of color in the general population and especially among student enrollments in schools. Accompanying these changes in demographics are growing demands that diversity be accepted as a fundamental element in all educational decision-making.

Common Bonds: Anti-Bias Teaching in a Diverse Society is written in this spirit. A persistent theme throughout is the reality of cultural diversity in all segments of American culture. In schools this translates into the need for educational policies, programs and practices to incorporate this reality. This theme is developed further through explanations of the wide range of diversifying factors and forces evident among student populations, including race, ethnicity, gender, physical and intellectual abilities, religion and languages, and how they do and should affect educational opportunities and experiences. That diversity should be an acknowledged, celebrated and determining factor in all instructional decision-making is the resoundingly clear message of all the contributing authors. They make this point vigorously, cogently and convincingly.

Another major issue in most current dialogues about educational effectiveness and pedagogical quality is the relationship between theory and practice. *Common Bonds* deals directly and impressively with this issue. Theory, research and practice are woven together to develop powerful and persuasive explanations of the whats, whys and hows of integrating cultural diversity into classroom teaching. The incorporation of case studies of actual classroom teaching in the narrative text of each chapter is one of the strongest features of this book. Allowing these case examples to tell their own stories in their own voices significantly enriches the rest of the content and brings a level of credibility to the arguments too rarely seen in educational publications. The case studies authenticate the theoretical ideas and general principles proposed by the authors by showing how they are carried out in the instructional behaviors and personal experiences of classroom practitioners.

A commendable feature of this book is its easy readability. The authors and editors write about complex and often controversial issues with clarity, conviction, passion and compassion, yet avoid sermonizing, being ostentatious or intimidating. They inform and teach while simultaneously affirming the creativity and accomplishments of others. They place their arguments, ideas and recommendations in the acceptable conceptual frameworks of cultural diversity, as well as the broader contexts of learning theories, pedagogical principles and new developments in instructional practice. The result is a book that is easy and enjoyable to read, an enriching and useful reference for education theorists and practitioners, and a commendable contribution to the body of scholarly and methodological literature on education for and about cultural diversity.

Contents

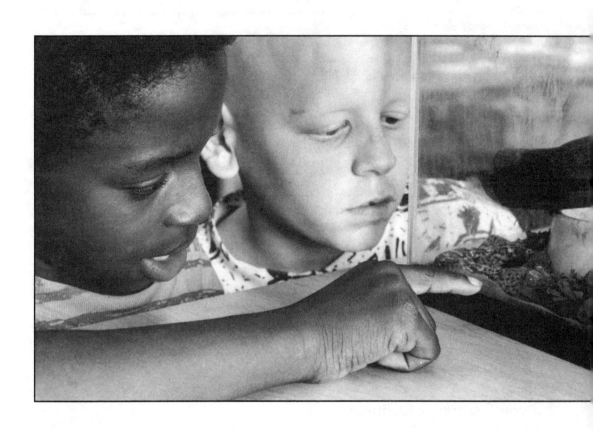

Introduction

Gary Kiger and Deborah A. Byrnes

Each year, American schools become more diverse. The varieties of cultural backgrounds, religious affiliations, socioeconomic classes, ability categories and language groups that characterize students in contemporary society pose an unprecedented challenge to teachers. As a result of immigration and high birth rates among lower socioeconomic status and ethnic minority groups, this diversity in schools will only grow in the foreseeable future.

In 1992, when the first edition of this book was published, African American children made up approximately 17 percent of the public school population. Latino children made up just over 12 percent. By the year 2000, public schools will experience a 16 percent increase in the number of Latino children, a 7 percent increase for African American children and only a 3 percent increase for white, nonHispanic children (U.S. National Center for Education Statistics, 1995). Moreover, the U.S. Bureau of the Census (Fernandez & Robinson, 1994) and the U.S. Immigration and Naturalization Service (1995) report that while the number of legal immigrants admitted to the U.S. has declined recently, the number of undocumented workers immigrating to the U.S. increased from 3.38 million in 1992 to well over 4 million in 1995. These undocumented workers and their children are likely not to speak English as their first language.

These statistics and predictions indicate only some of the challenges and opportunities that face classroom teachers today and in the near future. The diversity issues that we raised in 1992 are as relevant, if not more so, today.

There is a tendency in the popular culture to celebrate diversity. Writers and commentators often admire the rich blend of cultural differences found in society. While these observers have a point, it is equally true that diversity presents difficulties—especially in schools. How, for example, are teachers to communicate with, much less educate, children who do not speak English? What if a teacher's class includes 20 percent recent-immigrant, Afghan-refugee children, 15 percent Hmong children and 25 percent Salvadoran children? How, for example, can a white, middle-class, Catholic teacher be culturally sensitive to lower socioeconomic status or, say, Islamic children? Gender and ability differences among students add yet another important dimension to diversity in the classroom.

Schools traditionally served as places where minority students—whether they were ethnic, religious, gender or language minority-group members—were assimilated into the American culture, a culture typified as white, Anglo-Saxon, Protestant and male. Today, for a variety of reasons, the traditional view of schools as the melting pot for cultural differences among students is being challenged (Schlesinger, 1992). Various ethnic, language and religious groups often wage pitched battles for control of the curriculum and emphasis of their particular heritage in classrooms. Students with language problems or ability differences may sense that they are academically abandoned. Teachers are often faced with the dilemma of how to respect differences while finding some common basis to help children feel included in the classroom environment. Many teachers, not surprisingly, may feel ill-prepared to address their students' diverse cultural, personal and academic needs.

Purpose and Organization of This Book

The purpose of this book is to examine the growing diversity in schools in a constructive, empowering manner. Contributing authors identify various forms of cultural diversity and suggest ways that teachers can build inclusive classroom environments. The common theme is that while diversity poses difficulties, teachers can create an environment in which differences are recognized and accepted and simultaneously reinforce a common set of norms and values that bind students together. In addition, the authors suggest ways for enabling students to discard existing stereotypes and actively question and reject attitudes and actions not congruent with a pluralistic society.

Each of the six topical chapters deals with a different form of diversity in schools: a) racial/ethnic, b) religious, c) ability, d) socioeconomic class, e) linguistic and f) gender. Chapter 1 by Deborah A. Byrnes, "Addressing Race, Ethnicity and Culture in the Classroom," examines ways in which teachers can work toward racial and ethnic equity, social justice and democratic goals in their classrooms. She suggests two broad strategies. First, teachers should create "multicultural, anti-bias learning environments" that would include, for example, curricular materials that explore a range of racial and ethnic cultural content. The other approach is to teach schoolchildren to act assertively against prejudice and discrimination. Teachers have an opportunity to be role models by responding to issues of prejudice or discrimination that arise in student interactions, news reports or school materials. Although schools alone cannot eliminate racism in society, teachers can do much, Byrnes argues, to help children understand and accept racial and ethnic differences.

Chapter 2, "Living with Our Deepest Differences: Religious Diversity in the Classroom," by Charles C. Haynes, focuses on the limits and possibilities of dealing with religious issues. Haynes contrasts "teaching religion" with "teaching about religion"; the latter is encouraged, while the former is unconstitutional. Because religious beliefs involve ultimate values not easily compromised, it is not surprising that bitter debates rage over the place of religion in public education. While certain religious interest groups have sought to influence textbook selection and curriculum development in schools, it is equally true, Haynes maintains, that teachers and textbooks have too often neglected religion entirely as a topic of study and discussion. Haynes makes a compelling argument that religious differences can be respected and addressed in the classroom if democratic, constitutional principles guide the approach.

Mara Sapon-Shevin, in "Ability Differences in the Classroom: Teaching and Learning in Inclusive Classrooms" (Chapter 3), explores ability differences. She compares and contrasts the different kinds of abilities that characterize students; physical, perceptual and cognitive abilities are among the various dimensions schools use to differentiate pupils. Sapon-Shevin summarizes the arguments commonly heard for isolating students on the basis of ability: bright children may be "held back" by "slower learners" and special needs children cannot face the challenges of the regular classroom. She then reports the negative effects of separating children based on narrow notions of ability. Sapon-Shevin stresses the need to rethink our operating definitions of "ability" and to appreciate the research findings on the positive effects of current inclusive classroom environments.

In Chapter 4, "Class Differences: Economic Inequality in the Classroom," Ellen Davidson and Nancy Schniedewind focus on the effects of a student's socioeconomic status on his or her experiences at school. A child's class background correlates with his or her parents' attitudes about learning, classroom discipline and academic achievement. Also, a pupil's class background can influence interactions he or she has with peers and teachers (who are, by and large, drawn from the middle class). For example, peers can use class differences to ridicule one another. By not being sensitive to a child's family's lack of economic resources, teachers can unintentionally plan assignments that highlight class differences.

Davidson and Schniedewind show how addressing class differences in a constructive fashion involves more than being sensitive to differential wealth among students; it also involves addressing moral judgments based on class differences that may be made about children and their parents.

Linguistic diversity is the topic of Chapter 5, "Language Diversity in the Classroom." Deborah A. Byrnes and Diana Cortez, exploring the relationship between language and culture, maintain that language differences and language learning cannot be understood without appreciating the culture in which a language is embedded. They examine ways in which teachers can apply what they know (about language and culture) and enlist the assistance of classmates to teach English in a nonstigmatizing way to a language-minority student. Byrnes and Cortez also discuss the importance of exploring attitudes about language and language differences.

In the final topical chapter (6), "Gender Equity in the Classroom," Beverly Hardcastle Stanford examines the effects of sexism on schoolchildren. Stanford reviews research on gender differences in teacher-pupil interactions, academic achievement and student aspirations. She then offers suggestions to teachers on how to identify patterns of gender inequity in the classroom, which have a particularly insidious character. Even well-meaning teachers sometimes may find it difficult to recognize when they treat boys and girls differently. The encouraging theme in Stanford's work is the observation that "improved, equitable teaching can be brought about remarkably quickly."

Chapter 7 is an integrative work that explores the application of anti-bias teaching strategies to subject areas across the curriculum. James J. Barta, in "Integrating Anti-bias Education," provides specific activities for classroom teachers in each of several major subject areas. Barta points out that anti-bias teaching should not be viewed as something "added on" to the existing curriculum. Rather, anti-bias teaching should be inextricably linked to the presentation of subject-area material in math, language arts, science, art, music or social studies.

The concluding chapter by Karen Matsumoto-Grah is a checklist for classroom teachers of the important points raised by the authors. This useful device succinctly summarizes issues teachers need to bear in mind as they create inclusive classroom environments where common bonds are discovered and differences respected.

References

Fernandez, E. W., & Robinson, J. G. (1994). *Illustrative ranges of the distribution of undocu-mented immigrants by state.* (Technical Working Paper No. 8). Washington, DC: U.S. Bureau of the Census.

Schlesinger, A. M., Jr. (1992). *The disuniting of America.* New York: Norton.

U.S. Immigration and Naturalization Service. (1995). *Statistical yearbook.* Washington, DC: Author.

U.S. National Center for Education Statistics. (1995). *Digest of educational statistics.* Washington, DC: Author.

Chapter 1

Addressing Race, Ethnicity and Culture in the Classroom

Deborah A. Byrnes

We live in an increasingly ethnically, racially and culturally diverse society. Yet, schools often do little to prepare children to live harmoniously and equitably with such diversity. This chapter addresses the need for educators (most specifically classroom teachers) to take strong positions against prejudice and discrimination in schools and society and to actively educate for attitudes compatible with a racially, ethnically and culturally diverse democratic society.

Teachers often believe children, particularly young ones, are too protected and naive to have developed any understanding of, or judgments about, race and ethnicity. Consequently, discussions about such issues rarely occur in the classroom. Some educators fear such discussions would only call attention to differences that would otherwise go unnoticed. They may hope that if nothing is said, children will grow up thinking that race and ethnicity make no difference. While these teachers may be well-meaning, such beliefs ignore the evidence that: 1) children start developing attitudes about race and ethnicity at a very young age, as early as 3 or 4 (Katz, 1987); 2) skin color is the characteristic that can shape a child's experience more than any other, with the possible exception of gender (Phinney & Rotheram, 1987); 3) prejudice based on race and ethnicity remains a major social problem (Ponterotto & Pedersen, 1993); 4) avoiding discussions about race and ethnicity makes children easy targets of stereotypes to which they are exposed almost from birth (Pine & Hilliard, 1990); and 5) children must learn to understand and accept differences among various racial and ethnic groups and to actively fight against instances of racial and ethnic prejudice if we are to create a society based on equality for all (Davidson & Davidson, 1994).

If substantial changes are to be made to ensure that all racial and ethnic groups are treated equitably, every person involved with educating children must take an active role in the process. Although this chapter deals most specifically with the classroom teacher's role, the information contained here is relevant to *everyone* concerned with creating multicultural, anti-bias learning environments. While changing schools alone will not rid society of prejudice and bigotry, schools can make a valuable contribution toward resolving this pervasive and difficult social problem.

This chapter is divided into three sections. The first section contains recommendations for creating multicultural, anti-bias classrooms and schools. The second section is a case study that demonstrates how one teacher implemented many of the recommendations from section one. The third section lists resources on anti-bias education that will be of help to the classroom teacher.

CREATING MULTICULTURAL AND ANTI-BIAS CLASSROOMS

Multicultural and anti-bias education must be integrated into all areas of the school curriculum. To achieve this end, teachers must engage in self-reflection, professional development and personal growth. This section outlines effective ways teachers can work with children to reduce racial and ethnic prejudice. Additionally, recommendations are made for ways teachers can work with other adults to facilitate the development of multicultural, anti-bias learning environments.

Education That Is Multicultural and Anti-bias

All curricula should be anti-bias and multicultural. Unfortunately, multicultural education has too often meant simply adding teaching units about different cultures during special weeks or seasons of the year (Cushner, McClelland & Safford, 1992). Native Americans are studied at Thanksgiving time, African American culture around the birthday of Martin Luther King, Jr., and Mexican Americans on Cinco de Mayo. The rest of the year minority cultures are relatively ignored, reinforcing students' notions that nonEuropean groups are not really an integral part of American society.

When multicultural education is incorporated into a school's curriculum through the use of separate units, the rest of the school's curriculum often remains unchanged. All other subjects continue to be presented in the usual way, often in a manner that ignores minority cultures (i.e., subjects such as history, literature, science, art and music are taught only from an Euro-American perspective). The study and appreciation of different racial and ethnic groups must be integrated daily into all areas of the curriculum. Multicultural education must go beyond the presentation of cultural artifacts such as art, food and clothing, or the celebration of special holidays or famous people (Derman-Sparks & the ABC Task Force, 1989). Such approaches are often patronizing and deflect attention away from the day-to-day contributions and achievements of all individuals and groups.

Assessing materials. If educators are to integrate multicultural, anti-bias education into the entire school curriculum, they must carefully evaluate their teaching materials. All too often the resources that are readily available to teachers (e.g., textbooks, films, resource units) are strongly biased toward the Euro-American perspective (Tunnel & Ammon, 1996). Consequently, the contributions of people of color are devalued, giving students the message that Euro-Americans are superior. For example, many United States history books begin with the arrival of Europeans and then focus almost exclusively on the contributions of Euro-Americans. Other nonEuropean groups' contributions are rarely adequately acknowledged.

While some states are beginning to demand dramatic changes in the textbooks they adopt, many teachers are still left to their own devices to present a more multicultural perspective. For example, textbook coverage of Columbus often avoids the Native American perspective. A teacher wanting to discuss the treatment of the Taino or Arawak people is on her/his own (Tunnel & Ammon, 1996).

Teachers must carefully assess available materials to see if changes are needed. Visual aides should be examined to see if they present a diversity of racial and ethnic groups and are nonstereotypical. Children's books should be studied to see what percentage are about people of color and what messages are conveyed by the text and illustrations. Even children's books that have received prestigious awards may portray racial/ethnic minorities unfavorably, including Newbery award winners *The Matchlock Gun* (Edmonds, 1942), *Smoky, the Cowhorse* (James, 1927) and *The Slave Dancer* (Fox, 1974), which are available in almost all school libraries (Gillespie, Clements, Powell & Swearinger, 1992).

Textbooks should integrate the perspectives of minority groups into the subject being discussed. Do they incorporate the perspectives and contributions of Mexican Americans into the history of the Southwest? Is Islam discussed only in terms of violence and intolerance, with no exploration of broader commonalities with Christianity and Judaism (Wingfield & Karaman, 1995)? Recognizing the inherent bias in many educational materials is essential if changes are to occur. If more appropriate materials cannot be found, the biased materials should not be used without comment (i.e., they should be used to generate discussions on bias, stereotyping and discrimination).

Teaching about prejudice and discrimination. As part of establishing and integrating multicultural curricula into a school's educational program, prejudice and discrimination must be studied and discussed. Children should be encouraged to recognize the differences among and within various cultural, ethnic and racial groups while understanding that it is not the differences, per se, that create problems in society. Problems are created when one or more groups make serious value judgments about these differences. Multicultural education should not ignore the realities of these judgments. It is only through the recognition of such value conflicts that students can realistically hope to create change. Teachers and students should not view "color blindness" (i.e., ignoring or not noticing race or ethnicity) as the ideal. Encouraging students to be "color blind" ignores and denies the importance of race and cultural experiences with respect to each person's identity. Color differences do exist and we should not have to deny them for someone to be "okay." It is not the differences in race or ethnicity that we should ignore, it is the stereotypes and harmful prejudgments about such differences that we must teach students to recognize and work against.

It is important for students to understand that many people have suffered and continue to suffer as the result of irrational beliefs and actions (prejudice and discrimination). It is not enough to understand that injustice exists in the world; students must also learn that they can make a difference. By being aware of and sensitive to prejudice and discrimination, students can actively work against it in themselves and others. Children should be assisted in developing appropriate responses to instances of prejudice and discrimination (Byrnes, 1988). For example, letting a person who tells a bigoted joke know that one is offended, or assertively telling a peer that he or she is engaging in stereotyping behavior are important ways that students can take a stand against prejudice.

When addressing past and present instances of prejudice and discrimination, Euro-American children should not be made to feel personally responsible for what others have done. If discussions are not handled sensitively, Euro-American children may end up feeling personally blamed for many of the racial injustices being discussed and may respond defensively. Euro-Americans should not be stereotyped as racist any more than all people of any group should be assumed to have any specific characteristic. Euro-Americans throughout history have fought against injustice, prejudice and discrimination (e.g., Eleanor Roosevelt, Harry S. Truman, Gloria Steinem, Robert Coles) and Euro-American students should identify with such models.

Self-Awareness

To help children develop respect and understanding for racial and ethnic differences and become actively anti-discriminatory, teachers must also look closely at themselves to see if they are good models. Educators must examine their own knowledge, attitudes, behaviors and expectations. Multicultural, anti-bias education is often difficult to implement because classroom teachers' training or experience may not have provided knowledge of other cultures—their values, contributions and experiences. Likewise, many teachers may have little understanding of the relationship between race or ethnicity and power, and the injustices that prejudice and discrimination create (Robertson, 1987; Wardle, 1996). These deficiencies tend to be passed on to students and may also result in teachers being unaware of the racial and ethnic biases that may exist in their own classrooms (Lynch, 1987; Mallory & New, 1994). Only through self-education and self-monitoring can teachers avoid passing on the Euro-American ethnocentrism that is pervasive in our society and education system.

Seek out knowledge. Opportunities to gain insights into other cultures and to learn about the relationships among race, culture and power should be seized whenever possible. Such opportunities could be university classes in ethnic or multicultural studies, inservice workshops, lectures, cultural events, books or, most important, direct contact and interaction with people of other cultures. Involvement in groups whose main purpose is to protect the rights of others (e.g., National Association for the Advancement of Colored People, American Civil Liberties Union, Children's Defense Fund, Anti-Defamation League of B'nai B'rith) is another way to become more knowledgeable about social injustice.

Examine one's own cultural values and expectations. Teachers must also examine their own cultural values and expectations. Every teacher (as well as every student) brings his or her own cultural background to the classroom. Because most teachers and teacher educators in the United States are Euro-American, schools tend to benefit most Euro-American students, whose cultural patterns and styles are consistent with those of the majority of teachers (Anderson, 1988; Pine & Hilliard, 1990).

It is essential to recognize that differences in values and behavioral styles may exist, and that these differences may inadvertently influence one's attitudes and, consequently, behavior toward certain students. Teachers must check to see if they have an "ideal student" image that is similar to their own style and background. Such an image may result in categorization of students who are different in learning style, language or behavior as less able or disadvantaged (Twitching & Demuth, 1985). Such labels often affect the expectations a teacher has for a student and, consequently, can have serious ramifications for student achievement (Hilliard, 1989). Demanding less in terms of scholarship, waiting less time for responses, criticizing more and praising less, calling on students less often and less willingness to give students the benefit of the doubt are just some of the often subtle ways educators' own biases affect their responses to students who are different (Hilliard, 1989; Sadker & Sadker, 1986). To make things worse, a child can also pick up on a teacher's differing expectations and the effects may be incorporated into the student's own attitudes (Twitching & Demuth, 1985).

It is important to remember that most teachers are unaware of the degree to which they are treating certain groups of students differently than others (Sadker & Sadker, 1986). Teachers cannot assume their classrooms to be free of bias simply because they personally abhor discrimination. All educators need to examine their classrooms for subtle behaviors that may be based on culturally biased images and expectations.

Be actively anti-prejudice and anti-discriminatory. Educators have a responsibility to be models for their students. If they wish students to have tolerance for differences and to be active against bigotry, then they must examine themselves for these same qualities. In their teaching and personal actions, educators must demonstrate sensitivity to and respect for cultural differences and a commitment toward creating a pluralistic democracy that fights prejudice and discrimination. Are we willing to confront racist or ethnic discrimination when it occurs? Do we let others know that we find ethnocentric comments and actions unacceptable? Do our students see us actively addressing instances of stereotyping and bias? Do students perceive us as being sincerely interested in and respectful of the contributions made by the many ethnic and racial groups represented in our country?

Remember that respect does not imply value neutrality. An individual can respect and defend another group's customs (e.g., clothing, music, food, interaction style) without liking the specific practices or seeing them as options for himself or herself.

Creating Environments That Reduce Prejudice

In addition to integrating a multicultural perspective across the curriculum and being a positive model for students, a teacher can do much to foster respect and understanding and discourage prejudice and discrimination. The following strategies have been shown to be helpful in creating more positive attitudes toward persons of other racial and/or ethnic groups.

Cooperative interactions. One of the most effective ways students become more accepting of others is through cooperative-learning groups (Lynch, 1987; Pate, 1995). Research on cooperative grouping shows increased academic achievement, as well as improved interracial relations (Pine & Hilliard, 1990). Cooperative learning involves the heterogeneous grouping (by ability as well as by culture and gender) of students who then work together to meet a group goal. Such learning groups can be structured in several ways (see, for example, Slavin, 1990; Stahl, 1992). Regardless of the particular structure (e.g., Student Teams-Achievement Divisions [STAD], Teams-Games-Tournaments [TGT], Team Assisted Individualization [TAI], Jigsaw), cooperative-learning groups should always take place in ongoing, supportive environments where all participants have equal status. Maintaining a supportive environment requires that teachers monitor interactions within cooperative groups to ensure that some individuals are not being left out and to provide timely support for processing nonproductive group interactions.

In schools where the population is homogeneous, such grouping for cross-racial and cross-ethnic interactions is difficult, if not impossible. Any opportunity to have students engage in cooperative interactions with members of other groups, however, should be seized. Such encounters should incorporate the basic components of cooperative education. Members in groups should have equal status and the work or play should take place in a supportive, caring environment and be oriented toward a group goal. Sport teams and drama production groups that combine students from different communities and schools is one approach. Merely inviting members from other racial and ethnic groups to talk about their cultures should not take the place of the above type of interactions. Such impersonal, non-cooperative exposure to other cultures does little, if anything, to break down prejudice (Lynch, 1987).

Enhancing self-esteem. Creating classroom environments that promote positive self-esteem is another way educators can work against the formation of prejudices (Byrnes, 1988). A clear relationship exists between an individual's self-esteem and degree of prejudice (Pate, 1995). Children who have high self-esteem are less likely to hold prejudices than children who have low self-esteem. (This is not to say that the relationship is necessarily causal.) Some studies suggest that programs designed to increase self-esteem (a difficult task in itself) also bring about reduced levels of prejudice (Cook, 1972; Rubin, 1967).

Research tells us that children generally have higher self-esteem in school environments that foster security, acceptance, independence and responsibility and where warmth, praise and appropriate limits are consistently present (Curry & Johnson, 1990). Curry and Johnson, who share numerous strategies for fostering self-esteem in school environments, emphasize that children do not develop a genuine sense of human value through isolated "you are a winner" type of activities. Equitable, nurturing and challenging learning conditions that support self-esteem need to be present schoolwide. Efforts to develop such environments should be a priority for educators interested in reducing racial and ethnic bias among their students.

Developing cognitive sophistication. Research evidence also suggests that when children develop higher levels of cognitive sophistication they may also become less prejudiced. Individuals who are dogmatic, who think in sharp, dichotomous terms, are more likely to be prejudiced and act in discriminatory ways (see review in Pettigrew, 1981). If children learn to identify overgeneralizations and stereotypes and attend to meaningful social behaviors rather than biases, they may be less likely to develop prejudices (Pate, 1995). Thus, teachers should provide many opportunities for children to learn about prejudice and discrimination and to identify the faulty thought processes that underlie and perpetuate them. Students need to learn to be on guard for stereotypes and inappropriate uses of generalizations and categorical thinking in their own and others' thinking. (See the prejudice-reduction activity books listed at the end of this chapter for numerous activities on this topic.)

Notably, research on cognitive approaches and prejudice strongly suggests that factual information is not sufficient to reduce prejudice (Avery, Bird, Johnstone, Sullivan & Thalhammer, 1992; Pate, 1995). Lectures on prejudice and stereotyping will do little to help children be less prejudicial. It is necessary to go beyond content coverage of such topics as cultural diversity, human rights, tolerance and prejudice and consider ways to engage children in rethinking any prejudices and misinformation they may possess. We must involve students in discussions that help them to justify, express and reconsider their views in light of new information (Wade, 1994). These are the abilities of a cognitively sophisticated individual.

Increasing empathy for others. Increasing students' understanding of and respect for the feelings of others who are racially or ethnically different has also been shown to be helpful in reducing prejudice (Pate, 1988, 1995). Activities with a strong affective component, which elicits empathy, can help students see the world from the point of view of those from other cultural groups. Books, plays, short stories and simulations can be particularly helpful in helping students understand and empathize with the plight and fight of individuals confronted with discrimination and prejudice (Byrnes, 1988). Care should be taken that any resources used do not themselves unwittingly perpetuate stereotypes.

Working with Others for Change

Teachers who are committed to multicultural, anti-bias education must also work for change beyond their own classrooms. Encouraging their entire schools to develop a strong multicultural, anti-bias policy is an important step. Teachers' efforts to combat prejudice and discrimination are most effective when they are long term and supported by school-wide policies and practices (Davidson & Davidson, 1994; Lynch, 1987). Teachers and administrators should discuss what the school as a whole can be doing to create a learning environment that recognizes and supports a multicultural society. Part of this effort should be toward developing a school anti-racism policy explicitly stating that racial stereotyping, harassment and abuse will not be tolerated (Pine & Hilliard, 1990).

Involve parents. It is also important to involve parents and other community members in efforts to help children develop greater understanding of both the benefits and the challenges of living in a culturally diverse society (Derman-Sparks, 1989). Parents certainly should be involved in the development of any schoolwide policy. At the classroom level, parents can be informed of a multicultural, anti-bias curriculum emphasis during parent/teacher meetings and in newsletters. It is important to help parents understand that children need to develop healthy attitudes towards others who are different from themselves if they are to live and work in an increasingly pluralistic, democratic society. School-sponsored programs and activities designed to promote cross-cultural understanding are doubly advantageous if organized by a group of parents who are diverse themselves.

Diversifying the faculty. Any effort to emphasize multiculturalism in schools should also include a close look at the faculty makeup (Sleeter, 1990). Messages about the worth of all individuals, regardless of race or ethnicity, are hollow if students see only Euro-American teachers and administrators in their schools. Diversity among the staff provides an important lesson in equity to students, helps children develop respect and understanding of people from racial and ethnic groups other than their own, and provides access to role models for students of color (Pine & Hilliard, 1990). While many teachers have limited input into faculty hiring decisions, teachers should use what influence they do have to ensure the consideration and hiring of teachers who are members of minority groups.

Theory into Practice

In this chapter we have discussed the importance of education that is multicultural and strongly anti-bias. The case study below demonstrates how one teacher implemented anti-bias teaching strategies and processes in her own classroom. The case study illustrates how respect for racial/ethnic differences and a deep concern for fairness and social equality can be supported through incidental moments of teaching as well as in more formal curriculum approaches and strategies.

Amy Hafter, the teacher in the case study, does not shy away from addressing difficult topics with her students. She recognizes that her students are not "color blind" and that they pick up messages about race and ethnicity in their daily lives. In her democratically oriented classroom she uses such strategies as cooperative, interracial/interethnic group experiences; activities and questions that promote self-esteem, empathy and higher-level thinking skills; and literature that encourages students to understand and respect other cultures. She serves as a model to her students by actively fighting discrimination and being strongly committed to equity and social justice. She wants to instill in her students the importance of working toward a society where all people are respected and treated fairly without regard to their race or ethnicity.

CASE STUDY

When Amy Hafter began a new appointment as a 4th-grade teacher, she became aware of just how much she needed to address issues of prejudice and discrimination with her students. On the second day of school one of her students called another a "nigger." Amy was dismayed and anguished that this racial slur was used so easily by a 9-year-old. Consequently, she strove to make "respecting differences" a clear and consistent part of her teaching. According to Amy, "the more I thought about it the more I realized that prejudice and discrimination starts when children are young. We have to address it then."

At the time of this study Amy taught 4th-graders in a low-income community in Hayward, California. It was her fourth year of teaching and her third year at this particular school. She had 29 students, 20 of whom were male. Her students were from many different ethnic/racial groups. In order of numbers, from most to least, there were Euro-Americans, African Americans, Latinos, Afghan-Americans and Native Americans. No single group represented a majority. Only a few of her students were first-generation immigrants. All had good facility with English.

On my numerous visits to Amy's classroom, I was impressed by what I saw. Her students demonstrated respect for one another, concern for the way individuals were treated and interest in cultures other than their own; they worked cooperatively. In Amy's classrooms, principles of multicultural and anti-bias education are integrated creatively and successfully. This is the story of how one teacher helps prepare children to live peacefully and thoughtfully in a pluralistic society.

There were no desks in Amy's classroom. She chose instead to use large tables that fit into her cooperative-learning philosophy. Students kept their materials in tote trays under the tables. Every couple of weeks when the groups were changed (always by random assignment), students simply took their tote trays with them to their new tables. Amy feels strongly that students gain academically, socially and emotionally from working in cooperative groups. She also believes that such groups are an essential element of any program designed to help children accept and respect differences. Observing the groups, I was pleased to note that a new student, purportedly the child of Gypsies, was treated respectfully within her group even after giving a totally illogical response to a group math activity. While some of the students in her group were obviously a bit surprised by her response, no one teased her or made a derogatory comment. This was a good example of one of the basic premises of cooperative groups that Amy teaches her students. You cannot make a person feel uncomfortable about working in the group with you. If you do, you lose the right to work in the group.

Amy enhances her students' self-esteem, another important component of any prejudice-reducing program, by helping them to learn that their ideas are valuable and should be heard. She wants them to expect respect from her and from their classmates. Amy tries never to "shoot down" an opinion. In this way, she models respect for other viewpoints and encourages her students to think about issues and take risks. If a student shows disrespect for someone else's ideas, he or she is usually sent out of the classroom. This rarely happens, except among new students. As soon as she can slip away, Amy joins the student and asks him or her to reflect on why his or her behavior was hurtful and inappropriate and what behavior would be more appropriate. It does not take long for students to realize that respecting each other's viewpoints is taken seriously in this classroom. They also learn that their own viewpoints, in turn, will be respected. As Amy noted, "The students who have been with me all year [about two-thirds of the class] also help a lot in socializing the new ones."

Amy frequently spends time processing group interactions with her students. After a group cooperative project has been completed, students are often asked to talk about how well their group worked together. Did they respect each other's ideas? Was everyone given the opportunity to contribute? How were disagreements resolved? Students are discouraged from using individual's names in their comments. For example, the comment, "two members kept making jokes so it was hard to get everyone's ideas written down," is acceptable; "John and Sue kept us from getting done," is not. The students learn not to label their classmates; they learn to define situations in ways that help them resolve conflicts. Students discuss how it feels when people do not cooperate and they are encouraged to address such situations in their groups.

Any situation that involves an individual or group being discriminated against is discussed at length with the whole class. When a student recited a rhyme to some classmates that used racist language, for example, Amy talked with the student individually and then the whole class discussed why such rhymes are hurtful. Amy tries to get her students to discuss the issue as a group and adds her own views or clarifying points after they have listened to one another. In the above case she asked her students, "How did you feel when you heard it?" One student answered, "Mad! Because to call someone a 'nigger' means you think they're inferior and dumb."

The students did an admirable job of educating one another. Amy reinforced their reasoning ability by praising their group-discussion skills and their sensitivity to one another's feelings. Her students' growing understanding of the nature of prejudice and discrimination was evident in such responses as: "When T called me a 'nigger' it really made me mad. It didn't use to make me as mad when I heard that word. But now I know how my African ancestors were made slaves and it's different. I know what it means."

Amy rarely passes up an informal opportunity to address the importance of respecting cultural differences or to identify instances of prejudice and discrimination toward any group. In a mathematics lesson, for example, students practiced their graphing skills using M & Ms. Amy took the opportunity to discuss how M & Ms were a good example of what they had studied about people. Like M & Ms, we come in a lot of different colors on the outside but we are all the same inside. In a discussion of the popular children's film, *Land Before Time*, Amy drew parallels between the prejudice and discrimination some of the dinosaurs experienced with instances of racial and ethnic prejudice in the students' real world. At the individual level, when a student who was helping Amy after class commented that a woman with an earring in her nose looked weird, Amy used it as an opportunity to briefly comment on the cultural relativity of beauty. Pierced ears and bleached hair might be considered just as strange by people unfamiliar with those practices.

Discussions on respecting one another, accepting and enjoying differences, and taking an active stand against prejudice and discrimination are also purposefully integrated into many areas of the curriculum. Amy uses a literature-based reading program with books that reflect her purpose of helping students to develop empathy and understanding for others without regard to the color of their skin or their cultural background. Some of the books she used with this class were: *Freedom Train*, *Roll of Thunder Hear My Cry*, *Sing Down the Moon*, *Sign of the Beaver* and *Gold Cadillac*. All of these books have racial/ethnic minorities as the main characters and the plots involve important lessons regarding equality and respect for and understanding of cultural differences. Amy asks difficult questions of her students as they read these books. When they studied the book, *Roll of Thunder Hear My Cry*, for example, the class discussed what an "Uncle Tom" is and what it means in their own lives to "kiss up to someone" who is in power.

In the area of social studies, Amy avoids using the textbook whenever she can and instead uses materials that are more multicultural and less biased toward Euro-American perspectives. She admits this effort requires more work on her part, but it is the only way she can provide meaningful learning experiences that reflect the cultural composition of her students and their community. In a unit on the history of California, for example, she included a strong emphasis on the perspective of minority groups in the state. She also developed her own social studies lessons that address the internment of Japanese Americans during World War II. Fortunately, Amy's principal was supportive of her anti-bias curriculum.

After attending an excellent African American music-history concert and lecture, Amy's class integrated the new information into other topics they had been discussing. They discussed Martin Luther King, Jr., Harriet Tubman and others whose efforts made it possible for the students to have schools like their own, where all kinds of people could work and play together. Amy talks to her class about how strange she finds it when she visits her relatives who live in a community where everyone looks and acts the same. She shares how much more interesting she considers communities where there are many different types of people to get to know. Amy leaves no doubt in her students' minds as to her views on enjoying diversity and fighting against bigotry and prejudice.

When her students viewed the 12-part PBS video, *Voyage of the Mimi - Part II*, Amy frequently stopped the video and discussed topics related to individual and cultural differences. In one episode a character refers to the Mayans as "savages," not knowing that he was talking to a descendent of the Mayans. In the film, the person is deeply offended and the other character apologizes, stating he didn't know the man was part Mayan. Amy used this event as an opportunity to ask her students why people feel hurt when their culture is criticized. She asked if the comment would have been any more appropriate if no one who heard it was Mayan. Such discussions encourage students to think critically about prejudice and discrimination, to develop empathy for others and to engage in non-prejudicial verbal and nonverbal behavior.

Students regularly shared current events articles that confronted important social issues. Consequently, they frequently discussed such issues as homelessness, capital punishment and discrimination. One day a student brought in an article about the firing of an African American school superintendent in Selma, Alabama. Amy asked her students what they thought was happening in Selma. A discussion on racism ensued. Many of the students felt strongly that the superintendent probably was fired because he was black. They related the situation to other events of which their parents had spoken or to incidents of racial prejudice that they had observed or experienced. Amy was noncommittal with respect to her own opinion, but encouraged the students to express and support their own views. At the end of the discussion, one student summarized a solution, "I think the white and the black people should just be friends and they shouldn't be mean to each other. Even though we're different colors it doesn't mean we can't be friends."

In this case study I have described how one elementary school teacher strove to develop in her students a respect for diversity and a growing understanding of their responsibility to act in nonprejudicial and antidiscriminatory ways. Amy Hafter stands as an example of the many teachers who are working hard to create learning environments that prepare children to live thoughtfully and responsibly in a culturally pluralistic democracy. I thank her and her students for their contribution to this chapter.

There is no such thing as a neutral educational process. Education either functions as an instrument which is to facilitate the integration of the younger generation into the logic of the present system and bring about conformity to it, or it becomes "the practice of freedom," the means by which men and women deal critically and creatively with reality and discover how to participate in the transformation of their world. (Shaull, 1970, p. 15)

RESOURCES FOR TEACHERS

Prejudice-Reduction Activity Books and Materials

Byrnes, D. (1995). "Teacher they called me a_____!" Confronting prejudice and discrimination in the classroom. New York: Anti-Defamation League of B'nai B'rith.

Derman-Sparks, L., & the ABC Task Force. (1989). *Anti-bias curriculum tools for empowering young children.* Washington, DC: National Association for the Education of Young Children.

Duvall, L. (1994). *Respecting our differences: A guide to getting along in a changing world.* Minneapolis, MN: Free Spirit.

Ford, C. W. (1994). *We can all get along: 50 steps you can take to help end racism at home, at work, in your community.* New York: Dell.

Gabelko, N. H., & Michaelis, J. U. (1981). *Reducing adolescent prejudice: A handbook.* New York: Teachers College.

Guillean, A. (Ed.). (1991). *A world of difference: A prejudice reduction activity guide.* New York: Anti-Defamation League of B'nai B'rith.

Schniedewind, N., & Davidson, E. (in press). *Open minds to equality: A sourcebook of learning activities to promote race, sex, class and age equity.* Englewood Cliffs, NJ: Prentice-Hall.

Shiman, D. A. (1994). *The prejudice book: Activities for the classroom.* New York: Anti-Defamation League of B'nai B'rith.

Thomson, B. J. (1993). *Words can hurt you: Beginning a program of anti-bias education.* Reading, MA: Addison-Wesley.

Other Anti-Bias Sources and Materials

Anti-Defamation League of B'nai B'rith, 823 United Nations Plaza, New York, NY 10017.

Class of 2000: The Prejudice Puzzle (3 audiotapes and Teachers' Guide), National Public Radio Special Projects, 2025 M Street, NW, Washington, DC 20036.

National Institute Against Prejudice and Violence, 525 West Redwood Street, Baltimore, MD 21201.

Teaching Tolerance (biannual publication), Southern Poverty Law Center, 400 Washington Avenue, Montgomery, Alabama 36104.

References

Anderson, J. A. (1988). Cognitive styles and multicultural populations. *Journal of Teacher Education, 39*(1), 2-9.

Avery, P. G., Bird, K., Johnstone, S., Sullivan, J. L., & Thalhammer, K. (1992). Exploring political tolerance with adolescents. *Theory and Research in Social Education, 20*(4), 386-420.

Byrnes, D. (1988). Children and prejudice. *Social Education, 52,* 267-271.

Cook, S. W. (1972). Motives in a conceptual analysis of attitude-related behavior. In J. Brigham & T. Weissback (Eds.), *Racial attitude in America: Analysis and findings of social psychology* (pp. 250-261). New York: Harper & Row.

Curry, N. E., & Johnson, C. N. (1990). *Beyond self-esteem: Developing a genuine sense of human value.* Washington, DC: National Association for the Education of Young Children.

Cushner, K., McClelland, A., & Safford, P. (1992). *Human diversity in education: An integrative approach.* New York: McGraw Hill.

Davidson, F. H., & Davidson, M. M. (1994). *Changing childhood prejudice: The caring work of schools.* Westport, CT: Bergin & Garvey.

Derman-Sparks, L., & the ABC Task Force. (1989). *Anti-bias curriculum tools for empowering young children.* Washington, DC: National Association for the Education of Young Children.

Edmonds, W. D. (1942). *The matchlock gun.* New York: Dodd.

Fox, P. (1974). *The slave dancer.* New York: Dell.

Gillespie, C., Clements, N., Powell, J., & Swearinger, B. (1992). The portrayal of ethnic characters in Newbery award-winning books. *Yearbook of the American Reading Forum, 7,* 109-125.

Hilliard, A. G., III. (1989). Teachers and cultural styles in a pluralistic society. *NEA Today, 7*(6), 65-69.

James, W. (1927). *Smoky the cowhorse.* New York: Scribner's.

Katz, P. A. (1987). Development and social processes in ethnic attitudes and self-identification. In J. S. Phinney & M. J. Rotheram (Eds.), *Children's ethnic socialization: Pluralism and development* (pp. 92-99). Newbury Park, CA: Sage.

Lynch, J. (1987). *Prejudice reduction and the schools.* New York: Nichols.

Mallory, B. L., & New, R. S. (1994). *Diversity and developmentally appropriate practice.* New York: Teachers College Press.

Pate, G. S. (1988). Research on reducing prejudice. *Social Education, 52,* 287-289.

Pate, G. S. (1995). *Prejudice reduction and the finding of research.* (ERIC Document Reproduction Service ED 383 803).

Pettigrew, T. (1981). The mental health impact. In B. P. Bowser & R. G. Hunt (Eds), *Impacts of racism on white Americans* (pp. 97-118). Beverly Hills, CA: Sage.

Phinney, J. S., & Rotheram, M. J. (Eds.). (1987). *Children's ethnic socialization: Pluralism and development.* Newbury Park, CA: Sage.

Pine, G. J., & Hilliard, A. G., III. (1990). Rx for racism: Imperatives for America's schools. *Phi Delta Kappan, 71*(8), 593-600.

Ponterotto, J. G., & Pedersen, P. B. (1993). *Preventing prejudice: A guide for counselors and educators.* Newbury Park, CA: Sage.

Robertson, W. (1987). In-service strategies for teacher education. In T. S. Chivers (Ed.), *Race and culture in education* (pp. 96-105). Windsor, Berkshire, England: Nelson.

Rubin, I. M. (1967). Increased self-acceptance: A means of reducing prejudice. *Journal of Personality and Social Psychology, 5,* 233-238.

Sadker, M., & Sadker, D. (1986). Sexism in the classroom: From grade school to graduate school. *Phi Delta Kappan, 67*(7), 512-515.

Shaull, R. (1970). Foreword. In P. Freire (Ed.), *Pedagogy of the oppressed* (pp. 9-15). New York: Herder & Herder.

Slavin, R. E. (1990). *Cooperative learning: Theory, research, and practice.* Englewood Cliffs, NJ: Prentice-Hall.

Sleeter, C. E. (1990). Staff development for desegregated schooling. *Phi Delta Kappan, 72,* 33-40.

Stahl, R. J. (Ed.). (1992). *Cooperative learning in social studies: A handbook for teachers.* Menlo Park, CA: Addison-Wesley.

Tunnel, M. O., & Ammon, R. (1996). The story of ourselves: Fostering multiple historical perspectives. *Social Education, 60*(4), 212-215.

Twitchin, J., & Demuth C. (Compilers). (1985). *Multi-cultural education: Views from the classroom.* London: British Broadcasting Corporation.

Wade, R. (1994). Conceptual change in elementary social studies: A case study of fourth graders' understanding of human rights. *Theory and Research in Social Education, 22*(1), 74-95.

Wardle, F. (1996). Proposal: An anti-bias and ecological model for multicultural education. *Childhood Education, 72*(3), 152-156.

Wingfield, M., & Karaman, B. (1995). Arab stereotypes and American educators. *Social Studies and the Young Learner, 7*(4), 7-10.

Chapter 2

Living with Our Deepest Differences: Religious Diversity in the Classroom

Charles C. Haynes

Bitter conflicts over the role of religion in the classroom deeply divide the United States and pose a significant threat to the future of public education. Highly charged public battles, notably the "textbook trials" of the mid-1980s in Tennessee and Alabama and the ongoing disputes about prayer, equal access, religious holidays and other religion-in-schools issues, are only the most visible signs of a pervasive alienation from public education felt in many religious communities throughout the United States. Not since the 19th century "Bible wars" have so many citizens been so strongly convinced that public schools contradict their values, ignore their traditions and exclude their voices (Flowers, 1988; Glenn, 1988; Nord, 1995).

Tragically, citizens in communities throughout the U.S. ignore this threat and continue to shout past one another about "school prayer," "secular humanism," "cultural bias," "religious holidays," "values education" and the many other controversies that have made the public school classroom a battleground for conflicting religious values and world views. Caught in the crossfire are classroom teachers who are told to "educate for citizenship" and "teach appreciation for diversity" in a country where growing "tribalization" pits one group against another in the public square.

The religious differences so prevalent in the battle over public schools are now exacerbated by exploding pluralism in the United States. California alone receives nearly one-third of the world's immigration to the United States; minority-group members constitute a majority in public school enrollment (Hodgkinson, 1985). Sixty-seven nationalities are represented in the student body of a single high school in Miami Beach. A teacher in northern Virginia reports that 15 languages are spoken in her class, and her students often must serve as translators at parent-teacher conferences.[1]

In school districts across the country, teachers confront daily what other citizens choose to ignore: religious diversity in the United States presents the nation and the schools with unprecedented challenges. The language of pluralism may no longer be confined to the "Protestant, Catholic, Jewish" discussion prevalent in the 1950s. Religious pluralism today includes believers from all the world's faiths and increasing numbers of people who indicate no religious preference at all (up from 2 percent of the population in the 1960s to nearly 12 percent in the 1980s) [The Williamsburg Charter Foundation, 1988]. Islam, to mention just one highly significant example, will soon be, if it is not already, the second largest faith in the United States after Christianity generally. New populations of Muslims, as well as Buddhists and many other religious and ethnic groups, are entering U.S. schools in significant numbers (Haynes, 1990).

All these developments—religious and ethnic divisions, loss of faith in public education and exploding pluralism—summon us to rethink the role of religion in the classroom. At

---

[1] These are two of the many challenges of pluralism described by teachers in the workshops and seminars sponsored by The Freedom Forum First Amendment Center at Vanderbilt University.

issue is a simple, yet profoundly important, question: How will we live with our deepest differences? Our answer to that question may well determine the future of public education and the health of the body politic in the third century of our experiment in constitutional freedom.

ENDING THE SILENCE ABOUT RELIGION

If we are to live with our differences, we must acknowledge the importance of religious diversity even as we seek common ground. Efforts by school officials to ignore differences by excluding religion from the curriculum or by acting as though religious divisions do not exist (or do not matter) succeed only in producing false unity and false toleration. Elizabeth Kristol (1989) argues:

A healthy pluralism may in fact be characterized by the mutual respect that arises from a simmering of conflicting viewpoints and diverse senses of identity. . . . True tolerance means looking differences squarely in the eye and admitting the appalling fact that when other people seem to differ from us, this is because they actually believe their view of the world to be true. (p. A19)

Respect for differences and authentic toleration will be possible only when schools end what has been a virtual silence about religion and begin to take religion and religious liberty seriously. There is much irony in the fact that the public school, the very locus of the "culture wars," is the least likely place to find a discussion of the role of religion in history and society (Davis, Ponder, Burlbaw, Gorza-Lubek & Moss 1986; Haynes, 1985; Vitz, 1986). Ignoring religion and religious diversity has neither avoided controversy nor encouraged toleration—witness the ongoing court battles and endless fights over textbooks.

Silence about religion has only served to impoverish our curriculum and deny our students a full education. More serious still, we have given students the dangerously false message that religions operate only on the margins of human life and are largely irrelevant to human history and culture. Such misapprehension about religion promotes misunderstanding and intolerance, leaving students prey to distorted notions of how human beings have struggled with questions of meaning and value through the centuries.

The neglect of religion in the curriculum may be traced, in part at least, to the fear of controversy and widespread misunderstanding surrounding the Supreme Court rulings of the early 1960s in declaring state-sponsored religious practices in the public schools to be unconstitutional. What most educators do not understand (or choose to ignore) is that in those same rulings, the Court clearly indicated that teaching *about* religion is not only constitutional, but necessary for a good education.

Fortunately, events in recent years have brought about a dramatic change in attitudes about the place of religion in the classroom. States and local school districts from California to North Carolina are mandating more discussion of religion in the public schools.[2] Teaching *about* religion across the curriculum is finally being taken seriously: textbooks are changing, new supplementary materials are available and more opportunities for teacher education are offered each year.

A CIVIC FRAMEWORK FOR RELIGIOUS DIVERSITY

The growing consensus that study about religion is proper in public education offers teachers an unprecedented opportunity for promoting understanding and respect among people of all faiths and none. While this is easy to say (and for states to mandate), it is much

---

[2] The *History-Social Science Framework for California Public Schools*, adopted in July 1987, and statements by the state boards of education in North Carolina (1989) and Utah (1990) are three important examples of the new interest in teaching about religion in public schools. Many school districts throughout the nation are currently writing new policies and guidelines for teaching about religion.

24

more difficult to carry out in the classroom, especially in divided communities where some citizens are suspicious of any initiative public schools may take in study about religion. The risks associated with not learning about one another in an age of increasing pluralism, however, are much greater than the risks associated with including religion in the curriculum.

The first requirement for any teacher wishing to deal honestly and openly with religious issues in the curriculum and classroom is to give careful attention to the Religious Liberty clauses of the First Amendment to the Constitution: "Congress shall make no law respecting an establishment of religion, or prohibiting the free exercise thereof . . ." These 16 words provide the civic framework for teaching about religion and for handling religious differences in the public school classroom.

The United States Supreme Court has interpreted the First Amendment to mean that public schools may neither promote nor inhibit religious belief or non-belief. The public school curriculum may not, therefore, include religious indoctrination in any form (including hostility to religion). Such teaching would constitute state sponsorship of religion and would violate the freedom of conscience protected by the First Amendment.

Religious indoctrination, however, is not the same as teaching *about* religion or giving a fair hearing to religious perspectives. In the 1960s school prayer cases, which ruled against state-sponsored school prayer and Bible reading, the Court indicated that public school education may include teaching about religion. Writing for the Court in *Abington v. Schempp* (1963), Associate Justice Tom Clark stated:

[It] might well be said that one's education is not complete without a study of comparative religion or the history of religion and its relationship to the advancement of civilization. It certainly may be said that the Bible is worthy of study for its literary and historic qualities. Nothing we have said here indicates that such study of the Bible or of religion, when presented objectively as part of a secular program of education, may not be effected consistently with the First Amendment. (p. 203)

Beyond this baseline distinction between indoctrination and study about religion, certain key civic values and responsibilities flow from the First Amendment's Religious Liberty clauses. These values are so fundamental and enduring (and so vital to the classroom) that the new curriculum *Living with Our Deepest Differences: Religious Liberty in a Pluralistic Society* identifies them as the three Rs of religious liberty: rights, responsibilities and respect.[3]

Rights
Religious liberty, or freedom of conscience, is a fundamental and inalienable right founded on the inviolable dignity of the person. In our religiously diverse classrooms, it is essential that we emphasize this basic right as a cornerstone of American citizenship. Students must have a clear understanding that the rights guaranteed by the Constitution are for citizens of all faiths or those professing none.

Responsibilities
Religious liberty is a universal right that depends upon a universal responsibility to respect that right for others. Teachers must help students of all cultures and faiths to recognize the inseparable link between the preservation of their own constitutional rights and their responsibility as citizens to defend those rights for all others. In the language of the Williamsburg Charter curriculum, this is "the golden rule for civic life."

---

[3] The authors of *Living with Our Deepest Differences* are Michael Cassity, teacher and recipient of a 1989 California Educator of the Year Award; Os Guinness, former Executive Director of the Williamsburg Charter Foundation; Charles C. Haynes, Scholar in Residence at The Freedom Forum First Amendment Center; John Steel, Curriculum Project Director; Timothy L. Smith, Professor of History and Education Emeritus, The Johns Hopkins University; and Oliver S. Thomas, Jr., church-state attorney.

Respect

Debate and disagreement among people of different faiths and world views are vital to classroom discussion and a key element of preparing children for citizenship in a democracy. If we are to live with our differences, particularly our religious differences, *how* we debate is as critical as *what* we debate. As teachers deal with religious diversity in the classroom, it is vital that they teach a strong commitment to the civic values that enable people with differing religious and philosophical perspectives to treat one another with respect and civility.

Rights, responsibilities and respect, then, are the democratic first principles for addressing the role of religion in public schools. Teaching about religion is only one requirement of this civic framework. Teachers must also be careful to protect the religious liberty rights of students. For example, students have the right to pray alone or in groups, as long as such prayer is not disruptive of the educational process or coercive of others. Students have the right to share their faith with others, express themselves religiously in class discussions or projects, and distribute religious literature subject to time, place and manner restrictions. In secondary schools, students have the right to form religious clubs if the school allows other non-curriculum-related clubs (Haynes, 1994).

When teaching about the many cultures and faiths of the United States and the world, teachers must simultaneously teach and model the common ground—the rights and responsibilities outlined in the American constitutional compact. Done in this way, teaching about religion and recognizing religious liberty in the classroom become excellent opportunities for teaching respect for the universal rights and mutual responsibilities within which the deep differences of belief can be negotiated.

GUIDELINES FOR TEACHING ABOUT RELIGION

The principles of religious liberty remind us that although no religious consensus is possible in the United States, it does remain possible to develop out of differences a shared understanding of religion's role in public schools and public life. In 1987, concerned about the recurring conflicts over religion in the schools, a group of educational and religious leaders met in an effort to find common ground based on the civic values of rights, responsibilities and respect.

All of the groups represented, from the National Education Association to the National Association of Evangelicals, expressed great dismay over the divisive battles in the schools and courts and their devastating impact on public education. All agreed that the confusion about the role of religion in public schools has left school boards, administrators and teachers unprepared to handle religious differences and controversies.

Far too often, schools are asked to deal with societal problems without sufficient support and cooperation from the larger community. The time had come, the group decided, to assist local schools by reaching a national consensus about the constitutionally permissible and educationally sound role of religion in public education. Such an agreement would help to ensure that religious diversity is respected in the schools and that religious perspectives and values are fairly represented in the curriculum.

After a year and a half of discussion and negotiation, participants found that the principles of religious liberty can provide a common vision for the common good. For the first time, 17 groups from across the religious and political spectrum reached agreement about the proper role of religion in the public school curriculum. The Christian Legal Society joined with the American Jewish Congress. The Islamic Society of North America and the National Council of Churches agreed with the National School Boards Association and the American Association of School Administrators.

The group's guidelines, "Religion in the Public School Curriculum: Questions and Answers,"[4] stress the important distinction between teaching *about* religion, which is permissible, and religious indoctrination, which is prohibited by the First Amendment. The participants made a strong case for the natural inclusion of teaching about religion. In answer to the question concerning where study about religion belongs in the curriculum, the guidelines read:

Wherever it naturally arises. On the secondary level, the social studies, literature, and the arts offer many opportunities for the inclusion of information about religions—their ideas and themes. On the elementary level, natural opportunities arise in discussions of the family and community life and in instruction about festivals and different cultures. Many educators believe that integrating study about religion into existing courses is an educationally sound way to acquaint students with the role of religion in history and society.

Religion also may be taught about in special courses or units. Some secondary schools, for example, offer such courses as world religions, the Bible as literature, and the religious literature of the West and of the East. (Haynes, 1994, p. 10-1)

A year after the group issued these first guidelines in 1988, members reconvened to tackle the perennial problem of religious holidays in public schools. Despite widespread doubt that it was possible to reach consensus concerning the infamous "December dilemma," the group produced "Religious Holidays in the Public Schools: Questions and Answers."[5] That publication emphasized an academic, rather than devotional, approach in public schools. Consequently,

Teachers must be alert to the distinction between teaching about religious holidays, which is permissible, and *celebrating* religious holidays, which is not. Recognition of and information about holidays may focus on how and when they are celebrated, their origins, histories and generally agreed-upon meanings. If the approach is objective and sensitive, neither promoting nor inhibiting religion, this study can foster understanding and mutual respect for differences in belief. (Haynes, 1994, p. 10-2)

Teaching about religion and religious holidays may include use of art, drama, music or literature with religious themes if it serves a sound education goal in the curriculum. Use of religious symbols as examples of cultural and religious heritage is also permissible as a teaching aid or resource; such symbols, however, "may be displayed only on a temporary basis as part of the academic program" (Haynes, 1994, p. 10-3).

The most sensitive and controversial question concerning religious holidays in the schools is, of course, "What about Christmas?" The publication states:

---

[4] "Religion in the Public School Curriculum: Questions and Answers" is found in the publication *Finding Common Ground: A First Amendment Guide to Religion and Public Education*. This publication is available from The Freedom Forum First Amendment Center at 1207 18th Ave. S., Nashville, TN 37212. The sponsors of the guidelines are: American Academy of Religion, American Federation of Teachers, Americans United Research Foundation, Baptist Joint Committee, American Association of School Administrators, American Jewish Congress, Association for Supervision and Curriculum Development, Christian Legal Society, The Church of Jesus Christ of Latter-day Saints, National Association of Evangelicals, National Council of Churches of Christ in the USA, National Council for the Social Studies, National School Boards Association, The Islamic Society of North America, National Conference of Christians and Jews, National Council on Religion and Public Education, and the National Education Association.
[5] "Religious Holidays in the Public Schools: Questions and Answers" may also be obtained through The Freedom Forum First Amendment Center (see footnote 4). The quotes that follow are from this brochure.

Decisions about what to do in December should begin with the understanding that public schools may not sponsor religious devotions or celebrations; study *about* religious holidays does not extend to religious worship or practice.

Does this mean that all seasonal activities must be banned from the schools? Probably not, and in any event such an effort would be unrealistic. The resolution would seem to lie in devising holiday programs that serve an educational purpose for all students—programs that make no students feel excluded or identified with a religion not their own.

Holiday concerts in December may appropriately include music related to Christmas and Hanukkah, but religious music should not dominate. Any dramatic productions should emphasize the cultural aspects of the holidays. Nativity pageants or plays portraying the Hanukkah miracle are not appropriate in the public school setting.

In short, while recognizing the holiday season, none of the school activities in December should have the purpose, or effect, of promoting or inhibiting religion. (Haynes, 1994, p. 10-3)

Questions may arise in connection with holidays at many other times during the school year. A common example is when parents from some religious traditions ask that their children be excused from classroom activities or discussions related to particular holidays, even when the holiday is being treated from an academic perspective. Such requests often extend to holidays that many people consider to be secular but some religious groups view as having religious implications (e.g., Halloween).

Excusal requests involving activities or parties surrounding such holidays as Valentine's Day and Halloween are routinely granted. But what about requests for excusal from academic discussions of certain holidays? The guidelines read: "If focused on a limited, specific discussion, such requests may be granted in order to strike a balance between the student's religious freedom and the school's interest in providing a well-rounded education" (Haynes, 1994, p. 10-4). Parents will also ask that students be excused from school to observe religious holidays within their traditions. School policies should take into account the religious needs and requirements of students by allowing a reasonable number of excused absences, without penalties, to observe religious holidays. The guidelines note, however: "Students may be asked to complete makeup assignments or examinations in conjunction with such absences" (Haynes, 1994, p. 10-4).

These consensus statements provide local communities and schools with a broad framework for developing their own policies. When schools demonstrate that they take religion and religious liberty seriously through sound policies and substantive staff development, they receive strong support in their communities and can restore trust where it has been lost.

Yes, But How?

Now that widespread agreement exists that schools should teach about religion, the question facing teachers is *how* to do it? They are being asked to teach for the first time topics long ignored in the textbooks and controversial in the community. These teachers want and need straightforward advice on how to teach in this unfamiliar and sensitive terrain. The following answers to frequently asked questions offer practical approaches for meeting the challenges and avoiding the pitfalls of teaching about religion in a religiously diverse society.

When Should Teachers Talk About Religion and How Much Should They Say?

The best approach to discussions about religion is to place them within a historical and cultural context. Courses in history, literature, art and music on the elementary and secondary levels as well as discussions of family, community and instruction about holidays and cultures offer natural opportunities to teach about religious influences and themes.

How much is taught about the religion or religions of a particular historical period or culture, and decisions about which religions to include in the discussion, should always be determined by the academic requirements of the course. Teachers need teach only that which is essential to understanding the events or peoples under consideration.

Students should be made aware that any examination of religious traditions as part of a study of history and culture is necessarily limited. Teachers may find it helpful to inform students as to why particular religious influences and themes have been chosen for study. Students also need to know that much more could be said about the complexity and richness of religious traditions. Alert them to the fact that a wide diversity of opinion exists about religious events and ideas, not only among the various religions, but also within the traditions themselves.

How May Teachers Teach About Religion in a Way That Is Fair and Balanced?

We have already noted that teaching about religion must be done in an environment free of indoctrination. While a variety of religious perspectives may be presented, no religious or anti-religious perspective should be advocated by the teacher. When discussing religious beliefs, teachers can avoid injecting personal bias by teaching through attribution (e.g., by reporting that "most Muslims believe . . .").

It is important to remember the principle that fair and balanced study about religion must involve critical thinking about religion in history. Religion has been an integral factor in some of the best and the worst events in history. The full historical record (and various interpretations of it) must be open to analysis and discussion. In this regard, it is preferable to use primary sources where possible, enabling students to directly encounter and interpret the historical record.

But study of destructive or oppressive acts carried out in the name of a religious belief, however, should not be opportunities for attacking the integrity of the religion itself. All religious traditions have tragic chapters in which the ideals of the faith were not fully lived. These parts of the historical record can be taught without condemning a particular religion or religion in general. Attacks by teachers on religion or on the theology or practice of any faith do not belong in a public school classroom.

Be careful to avoid making qualitative comparisons (e.g., religion A is superior to religion B). Structural comparisons, such as pointing out that most religious traditions have scriptures and community worship, may be, however, a helpful way to organize class discussion. It may also be appropriate to compare and contrast the different perspectives religions might have on historical or current events.

What Are Some Common Pitfalls in Teaching About Religious Differences?

In an attempt to appear "tolerant" or "neutral" when teaching about religion, teachers sometimes, usually inadvertently, qualify religious truth claims as relative or reduce all religions to a common denominator—speaking of all religions as being "all the same" underneath their differences. For most religious people, however, such "toleration" distorts their faith and is anything but neutral. It matters very much to a Christian, a Jew or a Muslim what one takes to be ultimately true. These faiths, and many others, subscribe to absolute truths derived from the sources of revelation and authority in their traditions. The idea that all faiths are ultimately the same may be compatible with some world views, but is itself a philosophical or religious position. For a teacher to advocate this position in the classroom is a form of indoctrination.

Equally questionable are teachers' attempts to "explain away" religious faith as merely social or psychological phenomena. Such opinions may leave students with the impression that all truth is relative and that there are no absolutes. Teachers may present various theories of religion and introduce students to the social, economic and cultural context in which religions have formed and changed. It is first and foremost essential, however, to report how people of faith interpret their own practices and beliefs and how these beliefs have affected their lives historically—as well as how they affect people's lives today.

Public school teachers must strive to teach about the various approaches to truth without advocating one religious or philosophical position over another. Respect for differences is crucial if one is to understand the beliefs of the world's religious traditions. By taking care not to reduce or portray as relative the truth claims of religions, the teacher allows the student to learn how each faith understands itself.

Should Teachers Have Students Role-play Religious Practices?

Re-creating religious practices or ceremonies through role-playing activities is not appropriate in public school classrooms. Such activities, no matter how carefully planned or well-intentioned, risk undermining the integrity of the faith involved. Religious ceremonies are sacred to those who practice them. Role-playing may unwittingly mock or, at the very least, oversimplify the religious meaning or intent of the ritual. Re-creations of religious practices could violate the consciences of students asked to participate. A better approach is to use audiovisual resources and primary-source documents to introduce students to ceremonies and rituals of the world's religions.

What Should the Response Be When Students Ask the Teacher To Reveal His/Her Own Religious Beliefs?

Some teachers choose not to answer the question, stating that it is inappropriate for a teacher to inject personal beliefs into the discussion. Teachers of young children, in particular, have said they find this to be the most satisfactory response. Other teachers, not wishing to leave students guessing about their personal views and in the interest of maintaining an open and honest classroom environment, answer the question straightforwardly and succinctly.

The teacher who decides to answer the question by telling about his or her religious background should probably not do so at the beginning of the course or the year. Such questions are perhaps best answered once the teacher has had an opportunity to demonstrate how various religious and nonreligious perspectives may be discussed with sensitivity and objectivity.

When answering questions about personal beliefs, teachers may take the opportunity to note: "These are my personal beliefs, but my role here is to present fairly and sympathetically a variety of beliefs as we study the history of the world's great cultures. I only state my personal background so that you may better evaluate what I tell you." By answering the question briefly, with little elaboration or discussion, a teacher can offer a good lesson in civic values. Students learn that people with deep convictions are able to teach and learn about others' convictions in ways that are fair and balanced.

How Should Religious Views of Students Be Handled in the Classroom?

Teachers should not solicit information about the students' religious affiliations or beliefs. Nor should students be asked to explain their faith or religious practices to the class. Such requests put unfair pressure on students who may be reluctant to act as spokespersons for their tradition. Furthermore, students may be unqualified or unprepared to represent their traditions accurately. Students do have the right, however, to express their own religious views during a class discussion or as part of a writing or art assignment, as long as their statements are relevant to the subject under consideration and meet the academic requirements of the assignment.

It is the teacher's responsibility to clearly delineate at the beginning of the course or topic the civic ground rules for class discussion. The first principles of rights, responsibilities and respect ought to be in place as part of the civic framework of every class. These civic values support a classroom environment conducive to exploring a broad range of ideas and views in a way that is both respectful and nonthreatening. Students will learn that differences, even the deepest differences, can be discussed with civility, and that ridicule and prejudice have no place in schools or society.

Meeting the Challenge in the Classroom

U.S. public schools urgently need lessons for classroom use that address the principles and problems of religious liberty in a pluralistic society. The most comprehensive attempt to fill this need is the curriculum project mentioned earlier, *Living with Our Deepest Differences: Religious Liberty in a Pluralistic Society*. Using historical documents, literature and creative teaching strategies, this curriculum translates the three Rs of religious liberty into lessons for upper elementary, junior and senior high school students. Extensive lessons on each level provide a civic framework for understanding the place of religion in public life and demonstrate how practical dilemmas can be answered in terms of tolerance and mutual respect rather than bigotry and violence.

Living with Our Deepest Differences came about after leading educators asked the Williamsburg Charter Foundation, a nonpartisan, nonsectarian, nonprofit organization, to develop classroom materials that would teach the democratic first principles of rights, responsibilities and respect. A distinguished and diverse group of educators, scholars and faith community leaders served on the Editorial Review Board, chaired by Ernest Boyer, then President of the Carnegie Foundation for the Advancement of Teaching.

More than 150 teachers field-tested the curriculum during the fall of 1989 in five states (California, Maryland, Michigan, New York and North Carolina). Most of the teachers in the pilot program found the curriculum to be an excellent resource for teaching tolerance, understanding and appreciation for differences within the civic framework of religious liberty.

A response that typifies the enthusiasm and success of the pilot teachers came from Monica Glynn, a 5th-grade teacher in Portola, California. Monica infused her social studies teaching throughout the year with materials from *Living with Our Deepest Differences*. She tied the historical lessons of religious liberty to current events and connected the principles of religious liberty to other rights protected by the Bill of Rights.

Monica Glynn teaches in a classroom rich in ethnic and religious diversity. She used the historical documents and stories in the curriculum to help students understand how living with differences can and has been a source of continuing challenges and exciting opportunities. The first lesson of the curriculum, for example, focuses on the first Jews to arrive in America. Monica encouraged her students to think about who the "pilgrims" are today in the United States. She connected the struggle for liberty and economic security of today's newest Americans to the longings and motivations of immigrants throughout U.S. history.

She reports that her students began to see each other with new appreciation and respect. They were able, as she described it, "to put their feet in someone else's shoes" and to learn that "differences are special." Some of her students who occasionally felt stigmatized themselves (a Mexican-American boy, for example), began to see *themselves* with new respect.

Another aspect of the curriculum that excited students in Monica's classroom was the use of historical documents that allowed students to identify themselves with the people and stories of early American history. (All the lessons in the curriculum are history-based and contain primary source materials for distribution.) Documents, speeches, poems and songs help make history personal and immediate.

Monica used the "legacy" section of each lesson, which links a historical setting to its contemporary relevance "to bring the lesson home" through a discussion of current events. Themes of religious liberty and American pluralism in history come alive when students understand their connections to the principles that sustain the United States today as one nation of many faiths. On each grade level, lessons remind students of what is at stake in maintaining religious liberty principles. One of the "interest hooks" on the middle-school level is a chart showing that 25 of the 32 wars currently being waged in the world are rooted in religious and ethnic conflicts.

Each lesson also has a "parent connection," an activity to involve parents by giving them the opportunity to reinforce ideas taught in class. Before making these connections with parents through the lessons, Monica explained *Living with Our Deepest Differences* to parents at "Back to School" night and built strong community support.

RESOURCES FOR THE CLASSROOM TEACHER

Living with Our Deepest Differences is the most extensive curriculum available on religious liberty and freedom of conscience and one of the few new projects with lessons for upper elementary as well as for junior and senior high school students. The curriculum is now available on a cost-recovery basis from The Freedom Forum First Amendment Center at Vanderbilt University, 1207 18th Ave. S., Nashville, TN 37212.

Two books contain additional lessons for teaching about the role of religion in United States history. Although most of the lessons in these publications are designed for grades 7-12, many may also be used in grades 5 and 6.

Pathways to Pluralism: Religious Issues in American Culture contains 10 studies of significant religious issues in American history. Primary source materials are used in every lesson to present a variety of perspectives and to promote critical thinking. The authors, Robert Spivey, Edwin Gaustad and Rodney Allen, provide an accompanying teacher's guide with learning objectives, background material, teaching strategies and research topics. The book and guide are available from Addison-Wesley Publishing Co., 2725 Sand Hill Road, Menlo Park, CA 94025.

My own book, *Religion in American History: What To Teach and How*, contains a guide to teach about religion using archival documents and extensive historical background on the issues raised by the documents. I provide 13 facsimiles of primary source documents that may be easily reproduced for students (the book is spiral bound). Such documents as letters from Presidents Washington, Jefferson and Roosevelt, a Shaker diary, a nativist petition and a letter from an African American church to the Freemen's Bureau, all focus on the role of religion in U.S. history. Included is a list of 29 major religious influences in U.S. history as identified by Dr. Timothy Smith and a panel of historians and teachers. The publisher is the Association for Supervision and Curriculum Development, 1250 N. Pitt St., Alexandria, VA 22314.

Teachers who wish to give adequate attention to the world's religions when teaching social studies should have a reference book available that explains the basic concepts of each major religious tradition. *World Religions in America: An Introduction* edited by Jacob Neusner (Westminster/John Knox Press, 1994) and *The World's Religions* by Huston Smith (Harper and Row, 1991) are good examples of books that can help teachers supplement textbook discussions of world cultures.

Every teacher, especially in the elementary grades, would do well to have a calendar of religious holidays and ethnic festivals. Holidays and festivals can be valuable opportunities for introducing information about religions and cultures throughout the school year. Such calendars also alert teachers to their students' religious traditions and to observances that may result in student absences. The National Conference of Christians and Jews (71 Fifth Ave., New York, NY 10003) publishes a three-year calendar marking key religious and ethnic holidays. More elaborate calendars with photographs, "Ethnic Cultures of America Calendar" and "The World Calendar," are published each year by Educational Extension Systems (P.O. Box 259, Clarks Summit, PA 18411).

A comprehensive guide to resources for teaching about religion in U.S. history and world history is found in Finding Common Ground: A First *Amendment Guide to Religion and Public Education* distributed by The Freedom Forum First Amendment Center at Vanderbilt Univerisity (1207 18th Ave. S., Nashville, TN 37212).

EDUCATIONAL OPPORTUNITIES FOR TEACHERS

Even with the best curriculum materials in hand, many teachers do not feel fully prepared to teach about religion or to deal with religious differences among their students. Little is said about religion in most teacher education programs, and state mandates to include more discussion of various religions and cultures are not always matched by preservice and inservice workshops.

Fortunately, new teacher institutes and workshops that focus on religion are being developed in a number of states. The most extensive program is the California Three Rs Project (Rights, Responsibilities and Respect), a joint program of the California County Superintendents and The Freedom Forum First Amendment Center at Vanderbilt University. This project has teacher and administrator education programs underway in all 10 education regions of California. To find out more about these opportunities, contact Dr. Nicholas Piediscalzi, California Three Rs Project, 777 Camino Pescadero, Isla Vista, CA 93117. Other states, including Georgia, North Carolina, Tennessee and Texas have similar projects for helping teachers, administrators, school board members and parents understand the proper role for religion in the public schools. Information about these efforts is available from The Freedom Forum First Amendment Center at Vanderbilt University by calling (615) 321-9588.

The National Archives gives a workshop each summer on the use of primary sources in the classroom. A number of teachers use their time at the Archives to investigate and collect documents on the role of religion in American history. The Archives and its 11 field branches offer many additional services that support the use of such documents in teaching. For details about the summer workshop and other programs, write to Wynell Schamel, Education Branch, NEE, National Archives, Washington, DC 20408.

The National Endowment for the Humanities offers a variety of grants for teachers that may be used to learn more about religions. The Independent Study in the Humanities program provides a $3,000 grant to elementary or secondary school classroom teachers to conduct a six-week summer independent study in the humanities. Grants between $2,000 and $2,500 are given to teachers to participate in four- to six-week summer seminars on specific topics in the humanities, including religion. Master workshop study grants provide $5,000 to $30,000 to schools to conduct faculty-study and curriculum-development activities related to humanities education. For further information, as well as for proposal writing assistance, contact Carl Dolan, Coordinator, Access to Excellence Program, National Endowment for the Humanities, 1100 Pennsylvania Ave., NW, Room 802, Washington, DC 20506.

ONE NATION OF MANY PEOPLES AND FAITHS

Ignorance and contention about the role of religion in the public school curriculum is nothing new. For more than 150 years, Americans have fought about religion in the schools—and we have yet to get it right. The Protestant hegemony that characterized the early history of public schools has been replaced in many schools with silence about religion, censorship of religious perspectives and, in some instances, violation of students' religious liberty rights. Other schools have continued to promote the majority faith.

Neither of these approaches is consistent with the principles of religious liberty embodied in the First Amendment. The time finally has come to end both indoctrination and hostility by ensuring that religion is treated fully and fairly in the curriculum. Fortunately, we have, at long last, broad agreement across the religious and political spectrum that this should be done. In 1995, 20 leading religious and education groups (including the Christian Coalition and People for the American Way) agreed on the following description of religious liberty in public education:

Public schools may not inculcate nor inhibit religion. They must be places where religion and religious conviction are treated with fairness and respect. Public schools uphold the First Amendment when they protect the religious liberty rights of students of all faiths or none. Schools demonstrate fairness when they ensure that the curriculum includes study about religion, where appropriate, as an important part of a complete education.[6]

Our challenge now is to put this agreement to work in our nation's classrooms by guarding the students' religious liberty rights and by teaching about religion in ways that are constitutionally and educationally sound. By so doing, we prepare our children to live with even the deepest differences, and we help to sustain the boldest and most successful experiment in religious liberty in the history of humankind.

References
Davis, Jr., O. L., Ponder, G., Burlbaw, Gorza-Lubek, M., & Moss, A. (1986). *Looking at history: A review of major U.S. history textbooks.* Washington, DC: People for the American Way.

Flowers, R. (1988). They got our attention didn't they?: The Tennessee and Alabama schoolbook cases. *Religion and Public Education, 15,* 262-285.

Glenn, C. L. (1988). *The myth of the common school.* Amherst, MA: University of Massachusetts Press.

Haynes, C. C. (1985). *Teaching about religious freedom in American secondary schools.* Silver Spring, MD: Americans United Research Foundation.

Haynes, C. C. (1990). *Religion in American history: What to teach and how.* Alexandria, VA: Association for Supervision and Curriculum Development.

Haynes, C. C. (1994). *Finding common ground: A First Amendment guide to religion and public education.* Nashville, TN: The Freedom Forum First Amendment Center at Vanderbilt University.

Hodgkinson, H. L. (1985). *California: The state and its educational system.* Washington, DC: The Institute for Educational Leadership.

Kristol, E. (1989, September 25). False tolerance, false unity. *New York Times,* p. A19.

Nord, W. (1995). *Religion and American education: Rethinking a national dilemma.* Chapel Hill, NC: The University of North Carolina Press.

School District of Abington Township, Pennsylvania et al. v. Schempp et al., 374 U.S. 203 (1963).

Vitz, P. (1986). *Censorship: Evidence of bias in our children's textbooks.* Ann Arbor, MI: Servant Publications.

Williamsburg Charter Foundation, The. (1988). *The Williamsburg Charter survey on religion and public life.* Washington, DC: Author.

---

[6] Free copies of the full text of "Religious Liberty, Public Education, and the Future of American Democracy" may be obtained from The Freedom Forum First Amendment Center (see footnote 4). The sponsors of this statement are: American Association of School Administrators, American Center for Law and Justice, American Federation of Teachers, Association for Supervision and Curriculum Development, Carnegie Foundation for the Advancement of Teaching, Central Conference of American Rabbis, Christian Coalition, Christian Educators Association International, Christian Legal Society, Citizens for Excellence in Education, The Freedom Forum First Amendment Center at Vanderbilt University, National Association of Evangelicals, National Association of Secondary School Principals, National Congress of Parents and Teachers, National Council of Churches of Christ in the U.S.A., National Education Association, National School Boards Association, People for the American Way and Union of American Hebrew Congregations.

Chapter 3

Ability Differences in the Classroom: Teaching and Learning in Inclusive Classrooms

Mara Sapon-Shevin

Although we may talk about classrooms as "the kindergarten" or "the 3rd grade," and may assume similarities in the skills and interests of chronologically similar students, the reality is that all classrooms are heterogeneous. Typical classrooms have always served students who varied along any number of continua, including performance or ability. Many schools are now moving towards ever more *purposive* heterogeneity, attempting to limit the negative effects of tracking and recognizing the value of teaching children to interact comfortably with a wide range of people.

This philosophy, known as full inclusion (Stainback & Stainback, 1990; Stainback & Stainback, 1996; Villa, Thousand, Stainback & Stainback, 1992), is an outgrowth of the mainstreaming movement and represents a commitment to creating schools and class-rooms in which all children, without regard to individual educational needs or disabilities, are educated together. Rather than trying to "fix" children so that they can be fit back into relatively untouched "regular classrooms," inclusion aims to substantially alter general education classrooms so that they are more responsive to heterogeneous groups of learners.

Inclusive classrooms attempt to honor and respond to the many kinds of diversity that children bring to the classroom. Differences in race, ethnicity, gender, family background and religion are not dismissed in the name of standardization, but rather are appreciated and become part of the curriculum itself. Inclusive classrooms must also address differences in what is typically called "ability." Although one can never accurately predict any child's full potential or ultimate performance, children do differ in their skills, knowledge and competence. In traditional classrooms, these differences may lead to children being assigned to different reading or math groups, or being identified as "learning disabled" or "gifted." In reality, all children have abilities and strengths as well as areas in which they require more intensive instruction. As educators, we must make decisions about how to respond to these differences in educationally and ethically appropriate ways.

What are the challenges of teaching in classrooms that educate children who read well alongside those who do not read at all, children who learn quickly and easily with traditional methods as well as those who need intensive instruction or alternative strategies? The following exploration of these topics first examines some of the myths about ability differences and ability grouping that often perpetuate rigid, dysfunctional ways of teaching and instructional organization. Next, the author contrasts such beliefs with the realities of heterogeneity and mixed-ability groups, and explores some more appropriate ways to organize classrooms and instruction. A list of resources for implementing inclusive teaching concludes the chapter.

There Is Such a Thing As Ability

Many educators believe that each child has some fixed "ability level" that defines the best he or she can possibly do. Thus, we talk about children "not working up to ability" and sometimes, ironically, "overachieving" (that is, doing better than we predicted they would). Using these perceived differences as a basis we label children as "smart," "average" or "slow" or, for children whose differences appear more salient, "gifted" or "handicapped." We often adjust our curricula and expectations accordingly. In actuality, all people, including all children, vary along a number of dimensions, and it is generally not helpful to talk about ability as if it were a fixed, immutable potential for achievement. How well any child does is a function of many variables, including the nature of the curriculum, the child's self-concept, the flexibility and support of those who surround the child and the child's interest in the task. Therefore, if conditions were right, *we could all do better!* As Hunt (1961) noted:

It is highly unlikely that any society has developed a system of child rearing and education that maximizes the potential of the individuals which compose it. Probably no individual has ever lived whose full potential for happy intellectual interest and growth has been achieved. (p. 346)

Therefore, in some ways, we are all *underachievers,* and it makes sense for teachers to find ways to help all children achieve more and to create classrooms that nurture and support diversity. The recent work by Armstrong (1993) and Gardner (1983) on multiple intelligences helps us to recognize the many ways to "be smart" and that a single continuum of "ability" makes little pedagogical sense.

Students Learn Better in Homogeneous Groups

Some teachers still believe that by "narrowing the range" of abilities in the classroom, children will learn better because tasks will be more appropriate. Actually, despite the fact that many teachers continue to group students by ability, overwhelming research suggests that homogeneous grouping does not consistently help anyone learn more or better (Massachusetts Advocacy Center, 1990; Oakes, 1985). In fact, organizing children into high, average- and low-ability groups actually *creates* differences in what children learn by exposing them to different kinds of material. Although some children in high-ability groups may benefit from such arrangements, those who lose the most are those placed in average- and low-ability groups. Such grouping practices tend to compound racial, ethnic and economic differences in schools, as poor children and children of color are least likely to be served in enriched, gifted or high-ability tracks and are more likely to end up in vocational or low-ability groups.

Ability grouping also takes a serious toll on children's self concepts and on their opportunities to form meaningful relationships across groups. Children in the "slow group," the "low reading group" or what gets labeled as the "dumb class" are often painfully aware of the limited expectations adults have for them, and are subjected to teasing, ridicule and humiliation. Similarly, children who are put in top groups or removed to gifted classes are often labeled as "brains" or "nerds," and may find themselves isolated. Grouping children creates distance among them and tends to amplify and solidify whatever actual differences originally existed (Sapon-Shevin, 1994).

Teaching Is Easier in Homogeneous Groups

Teachers who have always organized instruction around three reading groups or a high-math group and a low-math group, find homogeneous grouping comfortable and familiar. But teachers who group homogeneously also complain about a lack of time to meet individual needs and about the low motivation and involvement levels of some students. By grouping heterogeneously for instruction, especially using models like cooperative learning and peer tutoring in which children learn to help one another, teachers often find that teaching becomes more enjoyable (Putnam, 1994; Sapon-Shevin, 1990; Thousand, Villa & Nevin, 1994). When heterogeneous teaching models are working well, children receive the benefit of peer instruction and motivation and the teacher's role shifts from management to instruction. Many teachers report livelier, more involved students and more challenging and exciting teaching experiences.

Children Are Cruel and Cannot Accept Differences

All of us have seen children teased and tormented because of their differences. We have all heard children call one another "four-eyes," "metal mouth," "dummy" or "fatso." Children also have tremendous capacity to become supportive and nurturing friends of classmates who are different from themselves. Yet children cannot develop such understanding, appreciation and social skills if they are kept isolated and segregated from peers who are different. Mere contact is not enough to promote positive responses to differences; teachers must systematically address student differences and appropriate interaction with their students *and* structure learning activities that encourage positive social interaction. The social climate of the classroom must be a *first* priority, not something to be "squeezed in" if time remains. Although children can be cruel, they can also be systematically taught to be caring, empathic and supportive of one another.

Parents Support Homogeneous Grouping and Tracking

Because many societal messages tell us that differences are bad and that people who are different must live and be educated separately, it is no wonder that many parents accept homogeneous grouping and the segregation of children who are different. Increasingly, however, parents of children labeled as "handicapped" are challenging the practice of placing their children in separate, isolated schools or classrooms. These parents want their children to grow up as part of the community in which they live, and this means going to school and playing with chronological peers. Many parents of "typical" children have also come to support integration or full inclusion within schools (Stainback & Stainback, 1990; Stainback & Stainback, 1996). This is particularly true as they see their children becoming comfortable with, and knowledgeable about, disabilities and differences. Even parents who initially expressed concern that the presence of children with educational challenges would "dilute" their own child's education have noted that, when conscientiously implemented, inclusive, regular classrooms do not lose any of their "rigor," but rather become more flexible, accommodating learning environments for all children.

Parents whose children have been labeled "gifted" are often conflicted. While they certainly want their child's educational and intellectual needs to be met and their child to feel accepted and valued, their choices may be constrained. Some parents feel (rightfully) that their child's unique needs cannot be met in the typical, workbook-oriented, lock-stepped classroom and that removal to a special class is the only solution. Other parents, however, worry about separating their child from his or her classmates; they do not want their child to feel stigmatized or overly different from other children (Sapon-Shevin, 1994). If and when parents can be shown "regular" classrooms that meet the individual needs of their child within an inclusive, accepting classroom community, the potential for parental support of heterogeneous grouping will be enhanced.

In order for teachers to teach and students to learn in heterogeneous classrooms, considerable attention must be given to classroom organization, curriculum design and community building. What kinds of teaching strategies are most appropriate and successful in heterogeneous classrooms? How can students learn to accept and understand one another's differences?

Cooperative Learning

Cooperative learning is one of the optimal ways to teach children with different abilities in the same classroom. Cooperative learning instruction involves children working together, helping each other to learn. Although much of the early work in cooperative learning referred to the importance of heterogeneous grouping, more recently the concept of heterogeneity has been expanded to address strategies for incorporating *all* children within cooperative learning, including those previously segregated in special classes or separate programs (Putnam, 1994; Thousand et al., 1994)

Of the many structured systems of cooperative learning, one method, called Jigsaw (Aronson, 1978), involves dividing the material to be learned into five or six parts and assigning students to heterogeneous five- or six-member teams. Each student is responsible for learning and then teaching his or her portion of the material to the whole team. Members of different groups who have been assigned the same portion of material meet in "expert groups" to study and discuss their section. Because each group member is responsible for all the material, all students must help each other learn; no one can sit back without participating.

The Jigsaw method can be used to teach many things: one 2nd-grade teacher assigns groups of five and gives each group member two of the week's ten spelling words to teach to the rest of the group. A 5th-grade teacher required group members to learn and then teach different parts of a unit on Africa. Group members specialized in the music, art, food, geography or history of the region. Paula Boilard, a band teacher, divided her jazz band into groups who became "experts" in the rhythm, dynamics, articulation and melody of a new piece. By learning the rhythm for all the instruments each member gained a much better sense of how the whole piece fit together. The band's harmony was increased in many ways!

Another way of organizing the classroom for cooperative learning is sometimes called "Learning Together" (Johnson & Johnson, 1975). The teacher assigns heterogeneous groups of students to produce a single product as a group. The teacher arranges the classroom to facilitate peer interaction, provides appropriate materials, constructs and explains the task so that it requires group cooperation, observes the students' interactions and intervenes as necessary. Students might be placed with a partner, for example, and asked to do a complex math problem. Each member must be able to explain the answer; they cannot just say, "Because Mike said the answer is 34." Therefore, higher-level students must work with and teach lower-level students. Larger groups of four or five might be asked to produce a skit, with different group members assigned to the writing, directing and acting, or to write a cooperative report.

Within this method, considerable emphasis is placed on teaching group members appropriate social skills to facilitate smooth interaction and cooperation. This can be done in various ways. Sometimes, one student in the group functions as the observer, recording the various facilitative behaviors of the group members. He or she might note, for example, how often each member talks, encourages others, asks questions or clarifies. At the end of the session, the observer shares this information with the group, so that all students can begin to understand which behaviors help a group succeed and how these behaviors can be developed.

An alternative way to build appropriate group social skills is to assign special tasks to each group member. If the group's task, for example, is to generate a list of ways the school could recycle waste products, one group member might be assigned the role of recorder (writing down what people say), one the role of encourager (making sure that everyone contributes), one the role of clarifier (making sure that everyone agrees with and understands what has been written) and one the role of reporter (sharing with the large group what has been recorded). These roles might be clearly described for the students on different cards, and the teacher could engage students in lessons on how to do each task: "What are some ways you could encourage other people in your group?" or "What are some clarifying questions you could ask your group members?"

Teachers can encourage class-wide cooperation in less formal ways as well. One 4th-grade teacher implemented what she called the "family rule." Students were seated in clusters of four desks; the rule was that no one in the group could ask the teacher a question unless he or she had first checked with everyone else in the group. Consequently, the teacher received relief from an endless stream of questions, and the students not only took active responsibility for helping their classmates find the right page, figure out the worksheet instructions and spell a difficult word, but also began to see each other as resources in many other ways. The teacher reported that children who were worried or upset about other issues (e.g., lost lunch money, a bully on the playground, a sick puppy at home) began to turn to one another for comfort and support.

Teachers also encourage support and cooperation by putting children in charge of more aspects of the classroom. In some classrooms, students take roll, do the lunch count, decorate bulletin boards, make decisions about scheduling concerns and orient classroom visitors. By providing ample opportunities for children to exercise leadership and make choices, a teacher can help children to see one another as more than "the worst reader" or "the best math student."

Unfortunately, for many teachers, cooperative learning has been reduced to something they "do" with (sometimes to) students for a brief period of the day or week. Formulaic, regimented systems of cooperative learning often predominate, taking away the impetus to make all aspects of the classrooms and students' experiences cooperative. We need to examine every aspect of the classroom—what we teach, how we teach it, how we organize and manage students, how we respond to questions, how we solve problems and how we talk about concerns—so that children learn and live a philosophy of mutual care and interpersonal responsibility.

Peer Tutoring

Another way to address different skill levels within a class is to arrange for children to be resources for one another, through peer tutoring or peer teaching (Thousand et al., 1994; Villa et al., 1992). Such programs can be arranged at many different levels, both within classrooms and across grade levels. In one school, every 6th-grader has a 1st-grade math "buddy" with whom he or she works three times a week. This system provides extensive one-on-one instruction for the 1st-graders, and the 6th-grade teacher has reported that even the "worst" math students in her class are showing a renewed interest and enthusiasm for mathematics. She has seen some of the 6th-graders doing extra work to prepare for their teaching, so they would "be sure to get it right." In other schools, 1st-graders read regularly to 2nd-graders who listen appreciatively, and 6h-graders assist in the integration process of children with special needs. Teachers report that when students are involved in the process of integration, the incidents of teasing virtually disappear and any infractions are dealt with by the other students. "Don't make fun of Jim, he has cerebral palsy and he talks fine and we understand him," is a typical remark made by the students to correct their peers.

Patty Feld, a teacher in a small rural school, organizes her students to help one another. Several times a week, the children participate in what she calls SHOA (Students Helping One Another). For a designated time period, children work together in pairs, with one child being responsible for helping the other; half the time Patty decides what the pair will work on; at other times, the student being helped is allowed to decide what kind of help he or she wants. All students read books at their own level. In weekly book-sharing time, students tell each other about what they are reading and learning. All students benefit from one another's learning, and reading-level differences are minimized by the cooperative sharing.

Teachers can arrange for students to help one another and become educational resources and sources of support in other ways. One teacher, who had a new record player and was anxious to ensure that all students learned to operate it properly, taught one little boy all about the machine. He learned which part was the tone arm, where the volume was adjusted and how to operate the machine gently. He taught two other children during the day, and checked them out on the process. Each of these children then taught two more, until the whole class knew the correct procedures. The record player was carefully attended at all times, and some of the classroom dynamics shifted by structuring situations where "high achievers" learned from nonreaders.

Another 5th-grade teacher kept four students in at recess to learn a difficult craft project, and then asked each of these students to work with his or her table mates to complete the project. Students began to see one another in a new light. New respect was created for children who were not typically "stars" in the class.

In order for peer teaching or peer tutoring to positively affect some of the typical status hierarchies within classrooms, teachers must be careful that all children get a chance to be the teacher or the leader and that no one is stuck permanently in the role of receiving help. In inclusive classrooms where the range of skills and interests is wider than usual, it is especially important that relationships be reciprocal.

One way to ensure this reciprocity is to broaden the kinds of activities and projects that children do throughout the school year. One teacher created a *Classroom Yellow Pages* that listed children's names, their areas of "expertise" and the ways in which they were willing to provide assistance to classmates. The guide included entries such as:

- LaDonna Smith: jump-rope songs and jingles; willing to teach double-dutch jumping and crossing over to anyone interested.
- Miguel Hernandez: baseball card collector; can show interested people how to start a collection, special cards to look for and how to figure batting averages and other statistics.

By encouraging students to look beyond some of the typical school subjects according to which children may rank and evaluate themselves and each other, she created new areas of interest, promoted peer interaction and broke existing stereotypes about "who was smart and who wasn't." Study of the multiple intelligences theory (Armstrong, 1993; Gardner, 1983) can help us to think more broadly about abilities and differences so that all students are valued for their strengths and supported in their areas of challenge.

Multi-level Teaching

In order to teach a wide range of students within one classroom, teachers need to rethink not only how they teach, but also what they teach. Instead of assuming that all students will be engaged in identical learning experiences for the same unit and evaluated according to the same criteria, the curriculum can be conceptualized as broad and inclusive. If the class is doing a unit on space, for example, the teacher can organize space activities and projects on many different levels. Children who have exceptional reading and research skills might be asked to write a report on the origins of the galaxy. Other children might be asked to draw and label the major planets in the solar system. A child with limited language skills might be required to be able to point to pictures of the sun, the moon and the earth in different arrangements. Every student would share their completed projects with the whole group, so that everyone benefits from the diversity of activities.

In one classroom that contained both students identified as "gifted" and students labeled as "mentally retarded," the teacher set up a school sandwich store. The students took teachers' orders for Friday's lunch and delivered their sandwiches on that day. All class members were involved in the project, but at different levels. Depending on their math skills, some children calculated prices according to ingredient costs, some figured out state and "classroom tax" and others did the actual shopping. Students whose educational objectives included functional skills, such as meal preparation, worked to make the sandwiches. Other students generated publicity and issued a monthly business report. By constructing a project like this, the teacher was able to engage all students in a collaborative project and still meet individuals' educational needs.

Teachers need continually to challenge the traditional curriculum and ask themselves: What does each child need to know? What aspects of this unit can be modified or adapted? Can students participate in the same activity with different levels of evaluation and involvement, or does an alternate, related activity need to be provided?

By asking these questions, teachers may find that they can achieve more flexibility for the whole class, and that modifications made with a particular student in mind can benefit many students. Patty Feld implements multilevel instruction by teaching across modalities. By including reading, writing, drawing and movement in her lessons, she is able to address the age and skill differences among her students. Classroom posters read, "We encourage our friends"; Patty tells students that questions are always okay. She not only encourages question asking, but also turns those questions back to the group. She says she has learned to ask open-ended questions that do not have right or wrong answers, and to wait for multiple answers. Often, a child who has not jumped into the discussion immediately later makes a contribution that enriches the conversation. Students who witness such exchanges realize that there are many ways to be smart.

Another teacher assigned one student a day to take a set of notes for the class (a carbon copy of personal notes) in order to meet the needs of a deaf student who could not take notes. The teacher later found that these notes were also helpful to students with learning problems who could not both listen and take notes, students whose handwriting left them with "holes" in their notes and students who were absent and needed to catch up. Another teacher, on the advice of the learning-disabilities teacher, began writing key words on the board and teaching them before beginning a new lesson. She found that all students benefited from this pre-teaching motivation and organization. Another teacher, in helping one student get himself organized by teaching him to use an assignment notebook and to check with peers for assignments, found that many students in her class could benefit from a similar system to keep themselves on task and on track. Such classroom modifications and adaptations benefit children's learning and also demonstrate that all students are valued. We do not abandon people who are having difficulties.

Teaching Social Skills
In order for cooperative learning and peer tutoring to be effective, teachers may need to address social skills. Teachers may want to provide direct instruction in ways to praise, offer encouragement and resolve conflicts.

One way of teaching such skills is by engaging students in a unit on giving and receiving help. Students can explore and practice ways of offering help (saying "Can I help you?" rather than "Let me do that, you're too short-dumb-slow") and ways of accepting and declining help gracefully (saying "No thanks, I'm doing fine," rather than "What do you think I am, dumb or something?"). All people need practice in these nuances.

Teachers can help students reflect on questions such as the following:

- What are three things I do really well?
- What are three things I have trouble doing?
- What are some ways I can provide help to people?
- What are some things I need help with, and what kind of help would I like?

The answers to these questions will show students, and the teacher, that everyone has skills and abilities, and everyone needs help in certain areas. Karen may be a whiz as a reader, but she may need help fitting into playground games. Carmen may struggle with her math, but she is great at remembering things and getting people and activities organized. Classrooms can become communities of mutual support if teachers promote respect for differences and provide multiple opportunities for students to see each other in many ways.

Patty Feld finds heterogeneous groups to be "a lot more like life," and she enjoys the interplay among different children. Patty addresses differences with her students directly. When some of the children wanted to play basketball, she engaged the students in a discussion of how they might equalize the teams so that it would be more fair and more fun for all; they also discussed ways of encouraging each other to play better. Students who were more skilled in the sport spent part of each gym period working with students whose skills were more limited.

Issues of friendship and exclusion can also be addressed directly. I recently worked with four teachers using Vivian Paley's book, *You Can't Say You Can't Play*. The book details how Paley, a kindergarten teacher, proposed a rule that children could not exclude one another and documented the subsequent discussions and implementation. These four teachers, a kindergarten, 1st-grade, 2nd-grade and 4th-grade teacher, implemented Paley's rule in their own classrooms and watched carefully as children wrestled with how to include a diverse group of peers in play and work activities. By making issues of inclusion a topic for discussion and observation, a focus of classroom concern, the teachers substantially altered their classroom climates and taught children new habits of the heart, new ways to think about reaching out and embracing others.

When children are working closely together, conflicts will inevitably arise that children must learn to resolve. One teacher set aside a walk-in closet where children in conflict can take themselves—not be sent—when they are having a conflict and need some time and space to work it out. Another teacher initiated what she calls the Problem Pail. Any students having a conflict can write what happened on a slip of paper and put it in the pail. Twice a week, she gathers the class together and fishes "problems" out of the pail. Each person involved in the conflict gets a chance, without interruption, to tell what happened. Then, the whole class generates possible solutions or strategies for resolving the problem. She often finds that the problems she fishes out were already worked out. The students sometimes come to the pail and remove a slip of paper because it no longer applies. With tattling removed as an option, some problems simply dissipate because it is too much trouble to write them down. Her class also keeps charts of problem solutions, a classroom compendium of solutions to conflict. When similar issues arise she is able to say, "What did we do last time something like this came up?" Students often refer to these charts on their own.

Teaching About Differences

Some teachers mistakenly assume that if they do not talk about the ways in which children in their class differ—do not comment on the fact that one child reads more slowly, that another talks with difficulty or that still another finishes math problems before anyone else—they will somehow avoid the comparisons and competitive evaluations in which children often engage. In truth, the opposite is more likely. When teachers do not directly address differences in skills and abilities, students receive the message that certain things simply cannot be talked about and their discomfort is likely to increase. How should teachers handle the differences in their classrooms?

First, teachers need to be careful not to send negative messages about differences. Star charts on the wall that indicate who is doing well and who is doing badly are not conducive to creating a classroom community that respects diversity. Most forms of competition in the classroom—spelling bees, awards for the "best team" and voting on the best essay—should be eliminated. Such competition is damaging not only to the student who does poorly ("We don't want Michael on our math team, we had him last week"), but also to students who consistently do well ("She thinks she's so smart just 'cause she got done faster than everyone else"). A good rule of thumb is this: if a visitor to the classroom can tell from the bulletin boards, the seating arrangement or wall charts who is doing "better" and who is "in trouble," then it is certain that the children themselves are also painfully aware of those differences and comparisons. Respect for differences is more likely to develop if all children contribute something to bulletin boards, students choose which paper they would like to display and room arrangements are flexible and inclusive. Avoiding negative comparisons, however, is only the first step, and it is far from enough. Teachers must find multiple opportunities to talk about and honor children's differences. When one kindergarten class integrated a student with seizures, no language and severe motor difficulties, the teacher engaged the children in an active discussion of the girl's limitations and how they could include her. The children themselves figured out ways she could participate in games, which aspects of the reading lesson she might be able to do and how they could include her in social activities throughout the day and on the weekend.

When children see that individual differences are supported in a noncompetitive classroom environment, they are free to celebrate the successes of their classmates without comparison. In one classroom I entered, a student rushed up to me and said, "Craig just got a new reading book and he can read real stories now!" Although the child who shared Craig's accomplishment with me had been reading for many years, he was able to recognize and appreciate Craig's important milestone. Confident in his own success and supported for his own accomplishments, he understood that every child in the room was working on what he or she needed in order to learn.

Teachers with heterogeneous classrooms who attempt to individualize instruction to meet children's needs will often be asked at first, "How come Noah doesn't do the same math we do?" or "When will I get to work on the computer like Nicole does?" How a teacher responds to such questions will do much to set the tone of the classroom; generally speaking, honest, forthright answers seem best. "Noah works in a different book because he's working on addition, and he's not ready for multiplication yet" or "Let's find a time when you can work with Nicole on the computer." Most who teach in inclusive classrooms report that, after a short period of time, children accept the fact that other children may be working on different levels or materials, and they often assist other students when they can. When both needing and giving help are treated as common, natural occurrences, then children can be accommodating of one another's challenges and appreciative of their accomplishments.

Promoting positive responses to diversity also means interrupting inappropriate responses swiftly and directly: "It's not right to call other people 'stupid'—what else could you say to Karen?" Teachers who tolerate name-calling and put-downs give children the clear message that such behavior is acceptable, or even inevitable. A teacher who says, "What can you do? Children are just like that" just does not feel able or inclined to address the social climate of his or her classroom. It is important that all educators carefully consider their own values regarding differences and what they want to convey to students.

Many excellent curricula for teaching about differences exist, some of which are included in the resource list at the end of this chapter. Students certainly need to know about the ways in which they differ in terms of skills, abilities and interests. It is equally important, however, for students to discover the ways in which they are alike. Stressing differences without talking about similarities can give students the idea that they have no common ground upon which to build relationships. When teachers are discussing student differences—who is good at what, who has trouble and so forth—they must also talk about the fact that all students are in school to learn, all persons have things they do well and things they do less well, and everyone does better with encouragement and support.

THINKING ABOUT INCLUSIVE CLASSROOMS

To create inclusive classrooms, teachers must think about what they teach, how they teach and how they structure interactions among students. If children receive consistent messages about the positive nature of diversity and the need for inclusiveness, all aspects of classroom life must reflect that commitment.

The Curriculum

Think critically about the kinds of display materials in the room. Do these materials model the belief that we all belong and can all contribute? Just as teachers will want to include books, posters and information about people of color and of various ethnic backgrounds in their classrooms, materials about people with differences and disabilities also should be included and integrated into all aspects of the curriculum. A unit on the five senses, for example, can include information on vision and hearing impairments. A unit on fairy tales can include a discussion of characters who feel different, such as the Ugly Duckling or Rumpelstiltskin, and a discussion of labeling and stereotyping. A unit on architecture can include information about physical accessibility to buildings and barrier-free designs.

Our Language

How do we talk about differences? Do we imply that it is better to be "all the same," or do we attach value to diversity? How do teachers refer to the resource room, how and how much do they explain why some children are chosen for the gifted program, and how do they respond to children who are struggling or failing? Children can also learn to be critical of stereotypes and misinformation about differences and disabilities. One teacher asked students to bring in cartoons containing words like "idiot" and "imbecile" and used them to lead a discussion about "smartness" and "stupidity" and how we should respond to such derogatory words and concepts.

Our Own Relationships with People Who Are Different

Does the teacher model respect for and inclusion of people who are different within his or her own life? It is hard for a teacher to convey the importance of including people who think or learn differently if this commitment is not represented in his or her own life. Some teachers who tolerate teasing and exclusion of children who are different are still working through their own past experiences with inclusion and exclusion. Gaining some clarity about the damaging ways in which we all were excluded periodically (or consistently) can be an important first step in increasing students' sensitivity. As we work to get ourselves, as teachers, surrounded by the networks of support we need, we can be more effective in helping our students do the same.

CONCLUSION

For classrooms to be inclusive, modeling respect and appreciation for all children, the areas identified in this chapter must inform all aspects of classroom life. Children learn what they live; if they are segregated by ability and skill for most of the day, an hour's lesson on respecting diversity is not likely to have a major impact. The typical school day or year provides multiple opportunities to problem-solve issues of inclusiveness. When one 5th-grade class that included a vegetarian child, a child who kept Kosher and a child who was Muslim wanted to plan refreshments for their party, the children brainstormed food choices that would allow everyone to eat comfortably. When a child using a wheelchair was not strong enough to lift himself out of his chair, the whole class became involved in a fitness and muscle-building unit to improve upper-body strength. Classrooms such as these send a consistent message: we are a community; we are all in this together; we will take responsibility for one another; we won't abandon people because of their difference or difficulties.

RESOURCES

Many excellent resources are available for both teaching children about differences and disabilities, and for structuring cooperative, inclusive classroom teaching.

Resource Guides for Cooperative Learning and Inclusive Teaching

These books may help teachers organize instruction and curriculum to promote positive peer interactions and the inclusion of children of various ability levels.

Aronson, E. (1978). *The jigsaw classroom*. Beverly Hills, CA: Sage.

Cohen, E. G. (1994). *Designing groupwork: Strategies for the heterogeneous classroom*. New York: Teachers College Press.

Dishon, D., & O'Leary, P. W. (1984). *A guidebook for cooperative learning: A technique for creating more effective schools*. Holmes Beach, FL: Learning Publications.

Gibbs, J. (1978). *Tribes: A process for social development and cooperative learning*. Santa Rosa, CA: Center Source Publications.

Johnson, D., & Johnson, R. (1975). *Learning together and alone*. Englewood Cliffs, NJ: Prentice-Hall.

Kagan, S. (1985). *Cooperative learning: Resources for teachers*. Riverside, CA: University of California, School of Education.

Moorman, C., & Dishon, D. (1983). *Our classroom: We can learn together*. Englewood Cliffs, NJ: Prentice-Hall.

Schniedewind, N., & Davidson, E. (1987). *Cooperative learning, cooperative lives: A sourcebook of learning activities for building a peaceful world*. Dubuque, IA: William C. Brown.

Sharan, Y., & Sharan, S. (1992). *Expanding cooperative learning through group investigation*. New York: Teachers College Press.

Tovey, R. (1995). Awareness programs help change students' attitudes towards their disabled peers. *Harvard Educational Newsletter, 11*(6), 7-8.

Resources for Creative Conflict Resolution and Class Climate

These books bring up issues of management, discipline and conflict resolution, all of which may require a different, more thoughtful approach in classrooms that are purposively heterogeneous.

Drew, N. (1987). *Learning the skills of peacemaking: An activity guide for elementary-age children on communicating, cooperating, resolving conflict.* Rolling Hills Estates, CA: Jalmar Press.

Fletcher, R. (1986). *Teaching peace: Skills for living in a global society.* New York: Harper and Row.

Kreidler, W. J. (1984). *Creative conflict resolution.* Glenview, IL: Scott, Foresman.

Levin, D. E. (1994). *Teaching young children in violent times: Building a peaceable classroom.* Cambridge, MA: Educators for Social Responsibility.

Prutzman, P., Burger, M. L., Bodenhamer, G., & Stern, L. (1978). *The friendly classroom for a small planet: A handbook on creative approaches to living and problem solving for children.* Wayne, NJ: Avery Publishing.

Ramsey, P. G. (1991). *Making friends in school: Promoting peer relationships in early childhood.* New York: Teachers College Press.

Resources on Cooperative Play and Games

These books can help teachers find ways to organize recreation and play so that children who are at different levels of skill can all have fun. These books contain suggestions for games and play that are inclusive and promote positive social interaction.

Fluegelman, A. (1976). *The new games book.* Garden City, NY: Dolphin.

Orlick, T. (1978). *The cooperative sports and games book: Challenge without competition.* New York: Pantheon.

Sobel, J. (1983). *Everybody wins: Non-competitive games for young children.* New York: Walker and Company.

Weinstein, M., & Goodman, J. (1980). *Playfair: Everybody's guide to noncompetitive play.* San Luis Obispo, CA: Impact Publishers.

Strategies for Promoting Full Inclusion Within Schools

These books describe the movement known as "full inclusion," which advocates reorganizing and restructuring schools so that all children, including those with disabilities, are included. They include many strategies for thinking about school reform and classroom organization.

Perske, R. (1988). *Circle of friends: People with disabilities and their friends enrich the lives of one another.* Nashville, TN: Abingdon Press.

Putnam, J. W. (1994). *Cooperative learning activities and strategies for inclusion: Celebrating diversity in the classroom.* Baltimore, MD: Paul Brookes.

Stainback, S., & Stainback, W. (Eds.). (1996). *Inclusion: A guide for educators.* Baltimore, MD: Paul Brookes.

Stainback, W., & Stainback, S. (Eds.). (1990). *Support networks for inclusive schooling: Interdependent integrated education.* Baltimore, MD: Paul Brookes.

Thousand, J. S., Villa, R. A., & Nevin, A. I. (Eds.). (1994). *Creativity and collaborative learning: A practical guide to empowering students and teachers.* Baltimore, MD: Paul Brookes.

Villa, R. A., Thousand, J. S., Stainback, W., & Stainback, S. (Eds.). (1992). *Restructuring for caring and effective education: An administrative guide to creating heterogeneous schools.* Baltimore, MD: Paul Brookes.

Teaching About Differences: Curriculum Guides

These resources offer strategies for talking and teaching about individual differences, including, but not limited to, disabilities.

Barnes, E., Berrigna, C., & Biklen, D. (1978). *What's the difference: Teaching positive attitudes towards people with disabilities.* Syracuse, NY: Human Policy Press.

Derman-Sparks, L., & the ABC Task Force. (1989). *Anti-bias curriculum: Tools for empowering young children.* Washington, DC: National Association for the Education of Young Children.

Neugebauer, B. (Ed.). (1992). *Alike and different: Exploring our humanity with young children.* Washington, DC: National Association for the Education of Young Children.

Schniedewind, N., & Davidson, E. (1983). *Open minds to equality: A sourcebook of learning activities to promote race, sex, class and age equity.* Englewood Cliffs, NJ: Prentice-Hall.

Children's Books About Differences

Many excellent children's books model diversity and inclusiveness. In addition to books that directly address disability/difference issues, more general books that address the multiple differences that exist in classrooms and society can be helpful in beginning a discussion with children.

Baker, K. (1990). *Who is the beast?* New York: Harcourt Brace and Company.

Barkin, C., & James, E. (1975). *Doing things together.* Milwaukee, WI: Raintree Publishers.

Brightman, A. (1976). *Like me.* Boston: Little Brown.

Cameron, P. (1961). *I can't said the ant.* East Rutherford, NJ: Cowan McCann Georgian.

Clifton, L. (1980). *My friend Jacob.* New York: Elsevier/Dutton.

dePaola, T. (1983). *Now one foot, now the other.* New York: Putnam.

Hazen, B. S. (1985). *Why are people different? A book about prejudice.* New York: Golden Books.

Heine, H. (1986). *Friends.* New York: Aladdin Books.

Henkes. K. (1991). *Chrysanthemum.* New York: The Trumpet Club.

Kasza, K. (1987). *The wolf's chicken stew.* New York: G.P. Putnam's Sons.

Schiff, N., & Becky, S. (1973). *Some things you just can't do by yourself.* Stanford, CA: New Seed Press.

Simon, N. (1975). *All kinds of families.* Niles, IL: Whitman.

Wolf, B. (1974). *Don't feel sorry for Paul.* New York: Harper & Row.

References

Armstrong, T. (1993). *Seven kinds of smart: Identifying and developing your many intelligences.* New York: NAL-Dutton.

Aronson, E. (1978). *The jigsaw classroom.* Beverly Hills, CA: Sage Publications.

Gardner, H. (1983). *Frames of mind: The theory of multiple intelligences.* New York: Basic Books.

Hunt, J. McV. (1961). *Intelligence and experience.* New York: Ronald Press.

Johnson, D., & Johnson, R. (1975). *Learning together and alone.* Englewood Cliffs, NJ: Prentice-Hall.

Massachusetts Advocacy Center. (1990). *Locked in/locked out: Tracking and placement practices in Boston public schools.* Boston, MA: Author.

Oakes, J. (1985). *Keeping track.* New Haven, CT: Yale University Press.

Paley, V. G. (1992). *You can't say you can't play.* Cambridge, MA: Harvard University Press.

Putnam, J. W. (1994). *Cooperative learning activities and strategies for inclusion: Celebrating diversity in the classroom.* Baltimore, MD: Paul H. Brookes.

Sapon-Shevin, M. (1990). Student support through cooperative learning. In W. Stainback & S. Stainback (Eds.), *Support networks for inclusive schooling: Interdependent integrated education* (pp. 65-79). Baltimore, MD: Paul Brookes.

Sapon-Shevin, M. (1994). *Playing favorites: Gifted education and the disruption of community.* Albany, NY: State University of New York Press.

Stainback, S., & Stainback, W. (Eds.). (1996). *Inclusion: A guide for educators.* Baltimore, MD: Paul Brookes.

Stainback, W., & Stainback, S. (Eds.). (1990). *Support networks for inclusive schooling: Interdependent integrated education.* Baltimore, MD: Paul Brookes.

Thousand, J. S., Villa, R. A., & Nevin, A. I. (Eds.). (1994). *Creativity and collaborative learning: A practical guide to empowering students and teachers.* Baltimore, MD: Paul Brookes.

Villa, R. A., Thousand, J. S., Stainback, W., & Stainback, S. (Eds.). (1992). *Restructuring for caring and effective education: An administrative guide to creating heterogeneous schools.* Baltimore, MD: Paul Brookes.

Chapter 4

Class Differences: Economic Inequality in the Classrooms

Ellen Davidson and Nancy Schniedewind

During 1983 to 1989, 55% of the increase in family wealth accrued to the richest half of 1% of families, while the lower-middle class and lower classes lost over 250 billion dollars of wealth. (Sanders, 1994, p. A2)

The gap between rich and poor is increasing steadily in the United States. At the same time, schools typically do little to help young people understand how economic inequality affects them—their understanding of their place in the world, their interactions with others and their ability to learn. We seldom provide students with the support they need to change that inequality. Yet education about class, and action to change class inequality, is necessary if we hope to provide equal educational opportunities for all and if we hope to maintain a democratic society.

Many Americans, especially those with sufficient income to live comfortably, do not think or talk much about class. The prevailing ideology that all Americans have an equal chance to succeed—and if some don't "make it" it's **their** fault—prevents people from examining economic inequality. Similarly, educators are seldom encouraged to reflect on the ways class bias affects them, their students and schools. We may have gone to a workshop or taken a course on dealing with racism or sexism in education, but how often have we been offered a workshop on classism? We can go into a good children's bookstore and request books that deal well with issues of race or gender and have our needs met. But what happens if we ask for books that portray families from a range of socioeconomic classes? Or ones that actually address class as an issue the way race or gender are addressed? While teachers may point to class background as a source of a student's learning or behavior problem, we are seldom encouraged to recognize and understand the discrimination that may accompany class difference and that requires collective efforts to address and change. We hope that the ideas in this chapter will initiate that process.

"Class" relates to a person's position in society as determined by money, power and access to resources and opportunities. Class background correlates with other factors related to schooling, such as expectations of the education system, support for various teaching approaches and attitudes toward discipline. "Classism" is the differential treatment of groups of people because of their class background and the reinforcement of those differences through values and practices of institutions such as schools. Schools, however, can and should be democratic institutions that provide all students with an equal chance. This chapter examines how class differences are perpetuated and how we can work to transform them.

There are many complex causes for the problems in schools that arise from the effects of class difference. Stereotypes of, and prejudices about, people from different class backgrounds affect the thinking and behavior of both teachers and students. When class prejudices and stereotypes are enforced by people and institutions in authority, such as schools, and perpetuated by cultural attitudes and values, classism is reinforced. In other ways, schools do not differentiate when they should—when students' socioeconomic backgrounds mean that they have diverse educational needs.

Success in institutions—schools, workplaces, and so on—is predicated upon acquisition of the culture of those in power. Children from middle-class homes tend to do better in school than those from non-middle-class homes because the culture of the school is based on the culture of the upper and middle classes—of those in power. The upper and middle classes send their children to school with all the accouterments of the culture of power; children from other kinds of families operate within perfectly wonderful and viable cultures but not cultures that carry the codes or rules of power. . . . To provide schooling for everyone's children that reflects liberal, middle-class values and aspirations is to ensure the maintenance of the status quo, to ensure that power, the culture of power, remains in the hands of those who already have it. . . . Many liberal educators hold that the primary goal for education is for children to become autonomous, to develop fully who they are in the classroom setting without having arbitrary, outside standards forced upon them. This is a very reasonable goal for people whose children are already participants in the culture of power and who have already internalized its codes. But parents who don't function within that culture often want something else. It's not that they disagree with the former aim, it's just that they want something more. They want to ensure that school provides their children with discourse patterns, interactional styles, and spoken and written language codes that will allow them success in the larger society. (Delpit, 1995, p. 25)

Class differences affect learning. Children from homes of lower economic status are likely to have fewer opportunities to develop the skills needed to succeed affirmed in schools that reflect middle-class values. Their parents are less able to give help on homework, provide many books in the home, pay for expensive trips or afford community-based educational and extracurricular opportunities—opportunities that children of more privileged class backgrounds have. What is of particular importance is that students themselves do not usually see these inhibitors or stimulants to academic success as contributing to their academic performance. Poorer students typically come to blame themselves and come to think of themselves as dumb, while privileged students develop a personal confidence and competence unconnected to its source in class privilege.

The effects of class on children's education is evident in the day-to-day experiences of children in classrooms across America. Structural arrangements within the class structure of American society perpetuate inequality in education. For example, housing and schools in America are highly segregated by class and race (Willie, 1985; Wilson, 1996). The most highly trained and effective teachers tend to teach in middle-class and upper middle-class school districts (Hacker, 1992). Moreover, schools that serve lower-income children are often characterized by unimaginative curricula, dilapidated buildings, violence, lack of parental involvement, little in the way of technological equipment and a distinct lack of extracurricular programs (Kozol, 1991; Wilson, 1996). All of these conditions negatively affect literacy, commitment to schooling and equality in society.

The effects of classism on positive social interaction are also evident in schools. As children move into the upper-elementary grades, and especially into middle schools or junior highs, they may find it harder and harder to cross class lines in social interactions, either in school or in the community. Barriers arise based on what students have, what neighborhood they live in, how their family lives, what they wear, what music they enjoy, their vocabulary and who their friends are. Classism thwarts learning, inhibits positive social interaction among students and ultimately reinforces inequality in society.

Americans tend to believe that schooling can help people transcend their class status. While this can be true for some individuals, schools overall serve to reinforce distinctions of class, race and gender. In fact, they reproduce the class structure by providing different materials, institutional practices and teacher-interaction patterns for students of different class backgrounds (Oakes, 1986). Schooling for working-class students is more likely to train them for routine and manual labor, while that provided to upper- and middle-class students involves more creativity and self-management (Anyon, 1981). Consequently, economic returns from school are greater for individuals who begin with more advantages (Jencks, 1979). This differential treatment affects student self-perception and consciousness as well. When upper- and middle-class students receive innovative, progressive instruction, they come to see themselves as capable of thinking critically and taking leadership. When poor and working-class students receive routinized instruction and authoritarian modes of discipline, they become conformist and accepting of routine in order to get by in school. Thus, both groups are prepared for the types of jobs waiting for them in a class-based society. Most educators are discouraged by these patterns, since we hope that our teaching can be a vehicle for class mobility. One way that hope can be realized is by better understanding classism and working to change it, and helping our students to do the same.

HEIGHTENING TEACHER AWARENESS ABOUT CLASS

Teachers are typically middle class; their values, part of the hidden curriculum, can affect the self-esteem of students from lower socioeconomic classes. Most discrimination on the part of teachers is typically unintentional, but it can be overt. We have not been encouraged to look at institutionalized practices that support inequality, particularly class bias. Therefore, when we start examining classism seriously, we may face surprising or unsettling realizations. We may come to realize, for example, that we have been unintentionally perpetuating inequality in our classrooms or our lives. While rarely easy to accept, such realizations can be challenging and hopeful; once aware of a problem we can change it.

We must begin by assessing how our own class backgrounds affect our views and ability to understand people reared under different circumstances. For example, it might be difficult for teachers from middle-class backgrounds, who grew up never worrying about having enough to eat or a roof over their heads, to understand and teach children who have such anxieties. Similarly, many teachers may have difficulty identifying and empathizing with the nagging, overwhelming self-doubt of working-class students (Lortie, 1975).

In any case, awareness of our own class backgrounds must be a conscious lens through which we examine our actions. We are often unaware of the subtle ways our own biases affect the classroom, such as the unintentional homogeneous composition of reading groups or our differing reactions to students' clothing. We can educate ourselves about the life experiences of those from other socioeconomic backgrounds and about classism in our society by reading, talking to others and reflecting upon what we see and hear. We can learn to be inclusive in how we work with our students, rather than perceiving a particular, usually middle-class, way of doing things as the only right way. (See interviews with teachers and suggested readings at the end of this chapter.)

In thinking about how to make changes, we might ask ourselves some questions. How does class bias affect learning in our schools? Do teachers have different academic expectations for children from different class backgrounds? Do teachers assume that some students will eventually go to college and others won't? Such expectations are subtly communicated to students and affect their own expectations. Ray Rist, in his classic study, explored primary teachers' assumptions about their students' economic status and how those assumptions affected time spent with, and expectations of, various groups of children. Anecdotal reports passed on to subsequent teachers resulted in the subtle tracking that began in kindergarten continuing throughout the years (Rist, 1970). Expectations matter!

It is useful to examine what teachers ask students to talk or write about. Are children allowed to bring in things that cost money for sharing? If so, in what price range? Sharing can be structured in creative ways that do not depend on money (e.g., sharing things children have made, stories or music from their own cultures, a skill they have learned from a grandparent or experiences they have had). Do we use examples of major consumer products in our lessons, reinforcing the idea that "normal" people have the desire and means to buy them? Do teachers ask students to write about summer vacations, assuming that all students travel with their families or visit relatives or friends away from home? Or do they structure such assignments to be inclusive and affirming to students without the privileges of such family outings?

A class could raise the money needed for field trips and school outings to ensure that *everyone* can afford to go. If the school is in a neighborhood where few people can afford to buy enough school-sold products to raise sufficient money, teachers can call upon local businesses to sponsor trips. Parents or older students can help write mini-grants for such sponsorship.

Examine the messages about "class" in textbooks and children's literature. Do texts focus on "famous people," usually those of privileged-class status, or are the accomplishments and hard work of poor and working-class people given equal focus and respect?[1] Look at the messages in storybooks. Do people who work hard always succeed? What message does this send to children whose parents are struggling hard and not making it? Do texts and stories implicitly blame poor people for their situation, or do they help children understand how some people have unequal opportunities because of their class background?

How do teachers deal with the class bias that emerges in social interaction among students? To tolerate name-calling or "put-downs" based on class bias (e.g., "What do you do, shop at Goodwill?") is to condone them. A strongly enforced norm of "no put-downs" is always in order. Do teachers themselves sometimes make assumptions about their students' class backgrounds based on superficial facts that may be misleading?

We can ask ourselves many other questions about classism in school. If schools have reading or other academic tracks, do most students in lower tracks come from lower income levels? Do most of the students in special programs for the gifted come from a privileged background? In classrooms, we have the opportunity to help children from different class backgrounds get to know each other by grouping students who might ordinarily distance themselves from each other. Teachers can promote both greater academic learning and a deeper inter-class understanding by using cooperatively structured/heterogeneous learning groups and teaching students about class bias to prevent reinforcement of old stereotypes. Students can learn to respect and affirm cultural diversity, creating an inclusive rather than exclusive atmosphere.

As we begin to answer some of these questions, we find many ways we can begin to deal with classism. One way is constantly to reflect upon our own assumptions and biases and adjust our day-by-day teaching to meet the needs of a diverse socioeconomic background population. Another is to educate students about class bias and provide opportunities for change in their classrooms and schools. As we reflect on and analyze that which occurs in our own lives and classrooms, we may be led to pursue more comprehensive changes as well. For example, we may ask how competitive norms and practices in schools and society contribute to the values and expectations that lead to class bias? Well-thought-out use of

---

[1]Good sources for teaching how poor and working-class people contributed to history and culture can be found, for example, in Zinn (1980) and Lerner (1973).

cooperatively structured learning in classrooms can improve academic learning for all and help students reflect on the ways competition supports inequality and cooperation contributes to equality (Schniedewind & Davidson, 1987).

HELPING STUDENTS UNDERSTAND AND CHANGE CLASSISM

Teachers can intentionally teach students about economic inequality and how to work to change attitudes and practices that reinforce classism. In their own classrooms and schools, students can examine how class bias may be perpetuated and work cooperatively to remove classroom-based barriers to equal learning, respect and opportunities for all. Students must become empowered to make changes within their control and develop a broader perspective on wider-reaching societal changes they will be able to help facilitate as they grow older. One sequential process for teaching students to understand and change many forms of inequality is laid out in *Open Minds to Equality: Learning Activities to Promote Race, Sex, Class and Age Equity*. Here we describe those steps in regard to educating children about classism. Details on most of these examples are available in *Open Minds to Equality* (Schniedewind & Davidson, 1983; 2nd edition, in press).[2]

Initially, it is crucial to build a supportive atmosphere in the classroom, one in which all children feel accepted and valued, both by the teacher and other students. At the beginning of the year, we should provide students activities for getting to know each other and developing trust. Before we initiate such activities, however, we must examine them for possible class bias and make needed modifications. Students should learn skills for working together. Some students may come to our classrooms with well-developed skills in cooperation, others may need a great deal of guidance. These skills must be taught, just as reading or math skills are taught. When students feel secure, accepted and respected by their teachers and peers, and feel empowered to share their ideas and work cooperatively with others, they can deal most effectively with an issue like economic inequality, which brings out many strong emotions.

It is also important to create a norm that affirms discussing class issues. Media bombards Americans with the message that if you are poor, it is your own fault and those who prosper have only themselves to thank. Students of a low socioeconomic status may have absorbed this message. Similarly, more privileged students may have acquired a self-righteous superiority. Students may not recognize such feelings in themselves. If they are aware, they may not be comfortable talking openly about them, especially in a mixed-class group. Therefore, we should set a tone in the classroom that encourages discussions of these issues. · The following statement can be adjusted to fit specific classroom situations.

All of us come from different family situations. For some, money isn't a problem but for others, having enough money for basic necessities is always a worry. Many of us fall in between. Some of us come from homes where our parents have had a great deal of education and others come from homes where a college education has not been possible. Some of us come from families who have easily been able to get what we want and make things happen the way we want. Other members of our class come from families who haven't had these advantages and don't have this kind of power. We will work hard to create a classroom where we understand, respect and value each other, whatever our family situation, and learn what we can do to help create a society where everybody has enough of what they need to live.

---

[2]The lessons described briefly in this section of the chapter are the following: "If Only We Had More Money," "Lizzie Gets Old Clothes," "What Are They—the ISMS?," "Letter from Sally," "Create a Mobile," "Ice Cream Sundaes, Apples or Raisins," "Our Textbooks: Are They Fair?," "Find That Classic Bias," "Are They Advertising More Than the Product?," "2192 Hours a Year," "Message in the Package," "I Want To Be," "Chicanos Strike at Farah," "Yes, You Can Be a Doctor," "From Fear to Power," "Textbook Alert," "Finding Better Books," "And We Wrote Them Ourselves," "Change That Classic Bias," "TV Turnabouts," "We Can Design Them Ourselves" and "Sharing Results."

As students become more comfortable talking about class issues, it is the teacher's responsibility to maintain guidelines for interpersonal communication and an ethic of care that protects their vulnerability. Teachers must be careful not to make assumptions about income, access to resources or values. They should, instead, teach students to gather data from which to work. Such activities can make excellent interdisciplinary lessons in mathematics and social studies. There are many simple ways to do this. Students can be asked to anonymously complete sentence stems about what they usually receive for birthday presents, what they do in their free time or how they receive medical care. Students can make drawings about what they hope to be when they grow up or what they would change about society if they could. Aggregate responses can be made into charts, bar graphs, pictographs or circle graphs and analyzed mathematically and socially.

Students need such accurate information about people of diverse class backgrounds and opportunities if they are to "get into others' shoes" and see the world from a different perspective. Role-playing a hypothetical situation in which a student is going to be left out of an event because of insufficient funds can be, with good follow-up discussion, an effective way to develop empathy with a student in that situation. Other students can then discuss times in their own lives when they, or other children, faced problems because of money shortages. The class can go further by comparing how economically disadvantaged students and economically advantaged students dealt differently with the role-play situation, and brainstorm strategies they could try in real life to deal more equitably with such a situation.

New words to define, name and discuss economic inequality and its consequences are important to students' growing awareness. They can learn about stereotypes based on class bias by working together to finish an open-ended story about the reaction of classmates to a student whose family might be evicted from their apartment. They identify the stereotypes and prejudices and write a different ending. After sharing endings, students discuss why some people stereotype others and what everyone loses by doing so. They share examples of class-based stereotypes that may have affected them personally and ways to combat such discriminatory preconceptions.

Children can learn to understand and identify institutional discrimination when shown the effects of prejudices and stereotypes practiced by those with more power than others or by institutions—like schools, families, the government, businesses. Discrimination against people because of the amount of money they have is a facet of classism. Concrete examples may help. A student may read a letter from a working-class high school student, expressing her disappointment at not being able to go on to college, with aspirations of becoming a doctor, because she must work to help support her younger siblings. After talking about that student's feelings, the class can discuss personal examples of having to give up something important to them because of the cost. Students discuss questions such as: Why did she have to give up hope of becoming a doctor because of lack of money? How should educational programs select students to become doctors? How should they support them? How do all Americans lose by the current situation of difficult access to a medical education? Such discussions give students new ways of understanding discrimination based on economic inequality.

Next, students are ready to examine how classism denies particular groups of people resources while supporting the success and achievement of others. They can learn to recognize the process of "blaming the victim." Those denied equal resources through institutional discrimination are often blamed for their lack of success. Students can examine how inequality can result from a *system* of institutional discrimination that distributes resources, opportunities and power unequally, rather than from deficiencies of *individuals*. Through experiential activities, students can feel what it is like to be expected to achieve without having access to equal resources and opportunities. In one such activity, the class may be divided into five groups, each group expected to make a mobile related to a topic being studied. Groups are given *unequal* resources for the project, but are evaluated by a *common* standard. After this experience the students share how they felt. They discuss ways people are expected to do equally well without having the same resources, power and money.

Students may then come to see how the privileges enjoyed by groups of higher economic status are directly connected to the lack of privilege for those of lower socioeconomic status. They can also learn about opportunities privileged individuals and groups have to foster change. In a simulated situation, two students are served ice-cream sundaes, representing the most privileged in the United States; most students receive an apple each, representing middle-class America; and 25 percent get only a raisin each, representing the poorest. The situation can be played out in a number of ways. A long discussion usually follows. Students first focus on how they felt and how they thought others felt. They discuss the choices they made and the choices they had but did not act upon. Was food shared? What questions did they ask themselves? What did they ask each other? A follow-up discussion could examine how this simulated situation reflects the current economic and food-distribution situation in the nation, how those with plenty of food are connected to the hungry and what can be done to change the structure of economic inequality.

Once students understand class discrimination better, they can examine their own environment—classroom, school, home, communications media and community—for class bias. Occasionally remind students that the intent is not to criticize, but rather to discover examples of inequality and understood that a great deal of discrimination is unintentional; only when people become aware of abusive attitudes can they change them.

Students can examine their school books in any subject area for classism. They can count how many people represented in the texts are middle or upper class compared to those of lower socioeconomic classes and determine if people from different classes are presented in different ways. Similarly, students can learn to pinpoint examples of class bias in other books they read and consider how books influence their own views about class. When students work in groups and compare findings, they can discuss what classes of people most stories address, try to determine the author's opinion of them and explore how students of different class backgrounds might feel when reading about characters whose lives are unlike their own.

Similarly, students can examine the communications media and their communities. Groups can be assigned to watch television commercials and newspaper advertisements to determine representation of people from different classes and what products they advertise. By analyzing television entertainment, they can determine the class and qualities of those portrayed and compare television families' economic situations to real conditions. Students also can analyze packaged products to determine how stereotypes of middle-class people are perpetuated as compared to those of lower-class people. What messages are being sent about superiority and inferiority? What effect do stereotypes have on real people?

Students can work to foster change by learning about people who struggle for economic equality, such as exploited workers who organized a strike in their factory. They can discover examples of more egalitarian living, working and learning situations, such as free access to medical education in Norway.

Students can act to make a difference. By engaging in collaborative efforts to make change, they develop a sense of personal and collective power. Providing them practice in assertively and standing up for their beliefs helps students build the skills and confidence to foster change. Students can then develop ways to educate others about class bias. By using their textbook analysis, for example, students can write to publishers about the class bias they discovered and request change. Or they may identify books that are not class biased and share that list with other classes. The class can discuss a story in order to challenge class bias—like *Scooter* by Vera Williams (see Books for Students). Students even can write their own stories that counteract stereotypes of low-income people. Suggest creating a problem in their story that a family might face because of unequal opportunities and resources and developing a creative solution that might include people making changes in the conditions that caused the problem. After peer review, students can present their stories in the form of skits, filmstrips or story boards for presentation to other classes and/ or displays on bulletin boards. They can create books for their school library that can be borrowed by students in other classes.

Students can re-create television ads to make them class fair and write letters to product-packaging companies with descriptions of preferable class-fair examples. Students can display their visual presentations on class bias in ways that will encourage others to think and ask questions. Change can be contagious.

NORMS AND PRACTICES THAT AFFIRM CLASS DIFFERENCES

Teachers can examine classroom and school practices that are class biased and work to create alternatives that validate children of all class backgrounds. By examining resources that might not get distributed to children equally, teachers can help students to develop ways to make their classrooms more equitable. How can we create a classroom where reading books and having access to books are possible for everyone? How can we help students—often those of lower socioeconomic status—who do not have the advantage of parents who read to them? Students of mixed-ability levels can read to each other in school, encouraging many students to be eager readers. Telling or reading stories to each other in school enriches children's sense of the breadth of literacy and affirms a range of lifestyles and cultures.

If family economic situations make it difficult for some children to order from book clubs, the class may devise creative ways for raising money to enable all children to have a reasonable number of books. A car wash, bake sale or raffle could be an effective means of raising book money. Local businesses can donate items for the raffles. Students can have fun with such a project while making book purchasing more equitable.

Also, teachers can find more equitable ways of charging families for field trips. An ice skating trip with free admission but a $2 cost per child to rent skates is expensive for children who do not own ice skates and free for those who do. Those who own skates are often the children in the class with more financial resources. By asking each family to contribute 50¢, the trip can be more accessible for all students.

Better-educated parents find it easier to help their children with schoolwork. How can teachers handle this discrepancy in a way that is helpful and affirming to all children and all families? Can we set up tutoring systems through which parents with particular skills help more than their own children? Can we organize cooperative groups where children from different class backgrounds work together and get help from any or all of their parents? How about restructuring some school assignments so that parents with skills not traditionally recognized by schools may have those skills affirmed and be able to help?

Academic tracking, most pronounced in secondary school, often makes its way into elementary schools. While educators used to think it served students and teachers well, tracking consistently has been shown to be counterproductive to student learning at all ability levels (Bellenca & Schwartz, 1993; Oakes, 1986). Perhaps more important, tracking also reinforces classism. Educators who raise critical questions about homogeneous grouping and tracking and work to institute educationally sound alternatives, such as cooperative learning, make important contributions to changing classism in schools. For these efforts to be effective, however, administrators, teachers, students and parents need to learn how heterogeneous grouping benefits all students through increases in academic achievement for students at all levels and improvements in social skills. Schools need parental and community support for these changes to last and truly serve all students.

My immediate response when someone says "class" is to get my back against the nearest wall and come out with this, 'What do you *mean* by class? Because I think it is a complicated issue.... . Class gets boiled down to issues of parents' income, issues of parents' education, but it's more complex.... . I prefer talking about 'access.' I ask myself, 'Is this a family that has had access? Access to schooling choices? Making health care choices? Advocating politically? Can this family come into a school situation and have impact on the school? Can they get what they need and want?' There's certainly something that's typical of middle-class kids in school and atypical of kids who are poor kids, kids for whom the United States is a new country—language issues play into it. So it's not as simple as income or parent education. (Davidson, E. [1990, July] interview with Judy Richards, Graham-Parks School, Cambridge, MA)

Dealing with day-to-day class issues in the classroom is complex. Judy Richards and Alma Wright, two experienced teachers, actively address class issues in their classroom cultures and daily teaching. Their clear beliefs about how best to work with a diverse socioeconomic population can help us better understand how individual teachers can handle these issues. In addition to an overall framework, each has developed many specific strategies. By comparing and contrasting their views, we can get a more complete picture.

Judy Richards teaches 3rd and 4th grades in an alternative public school in Cambridge, Massachusetts. She is white and comes from a working-class background. Her students are approximately one-third black Haitian, generally lower income; one-third white middle class or professional; and one-third African American or white working class.

Alma Wright has taught 1st and 2nd grades for 20 years at the Trotter School in Boston. Trotter, like many other schools in the city, is 60 percent African American, 20 percent Latino and 20 percent white. The African American and Latino students are primarily working class or poor; many students of color from professional homes in Boston go to private schools or participate in a program that buses them out to white suburban schools. Alma reports that most of the African American and Latino children live in housing projects and come from single-family homes. The white children in her class are primarily from middle-class homes with professional parents. Many white children from working-class homes attend parochial schools. Alma herself is African American and from a low-income background.

Judy and Alma point out that in order to create a classroom that is as free from classism as possible and affirms all children without regard to their class backgrounds, teachers must be aware of class issues and consistently look at how their actions affect children of varied classes. This means examining expectations, both covert and overt, being careful not to make assumptions about lifestyles and beliefs.

Values

Judy views schools as places where middle-class values and culture are constantly reaffirmed. Middle-class families support and perpetuate school values and, thus, children from these homes receive affirmation from their teachers because their home values are similar to school values. In contrast, teachers often judge and condemn poor and working-class families when their values and choices are different from those at school.

For example, Judy asks, "How often do we judge parental behavior as a righteous choice or not righteous choice? How is that tied into our behaviors with our students? What message do students get from our judgments?" Judgments about the class implications in language—grammar, vocabulary and syntax—come up repeatedly in the classroom. Judy recounts a time when she heard a student say to a teacher, "Miss, I ain't got no pencil." Instead of providing or not providing the pencil, the teacher used this as an opportunity to ridicule the student's language and emphasize that home language was not appropriate at school. By defining language as "only-for-home language," Judy believes school becomes a place where the student does not feel accepted or respected when it should be a place where the student feels he or she can succeed.

Inclusive Rather Than Selective

Judy says that "not condemning" a particular lifestyle is definitely not enough; teachers must actively *affirm* a diversity of lifestyles. Judy's classroom is inclusive rather than selective. She invites parents to participate actively in her classroom, providing varied opportunities that appeal to different parents. A core group of parents regularly volunteers to help with the Friday morning problem-solving sessions. These are almost entirely white, middle-class parents. Judy attributes this homogeneity primarily to the fact that these parents have professional jobs that allow them flexibility in scheduling. She also recognizes that her Friday mornings are high powered in a particular way that is attractive to well-educated, middle-class parents who have confidence in their backgrounds and abilities, but possibly intimidating to working-class parents who have not had access to education. She finds, however, that other parents from varied classes come to read to children, have children read aloud to them and participate in "open elective" time when a range of activities is offered.

I remember a woman who could tell wonderful stories to kids. If reading and writing were your criteria for literacy, she was illiterate. She had grown up in the Fernald School (a school for developmentally delayed people). But she would tell kids about animals. When her daughter learned to read, she really became interested in learning to read and went to the adult learning center.

When Judy conducted a theme on the local area, all parents could contribute. Some came from families who had lived in the area for generations and could share many stories. Others were recent immigrants who could talk about why they moved to the area. All these contributions were valuable to the children's understanding.

Judy modified her Friday morning problem-solving groups to be more inclusive. Children in heterogeneous groups of five meet weekly to solve non-routine mathematics problems. One she used for a number of years is this: "You go to the stream with a three-liter container and a seven-liter container. You want to come back with exactly five liters of water. How do you do it?" Judy "repackaged" this mathematics problem by using a Haitian folk tale that the children know in which a girl makes friends with a fish and thus gets clearer water than her brother. Judy uses the names of the girl and boy and their mother and incorporates their personalities in explaining what is wanted in the mathematics problem. By changing the problem in this manner, the middle-class children were no longer the dominant forces in the problem-solving groups. The Haitian children became the "experts" and leaders in their groups.

By changing the cultural and class bias of the problem, Judy also shifted the perceptions about her students' apparent academic abilities. Concerning the implications of this shift, Judy has advice for other teachers:

Certainly be very careful that when you design novel groups or math groups . . . that you look at the design of them and you say, 'Does this group have any diversity in it?' How can you rearrange it so it's not skill groups? Can you have a reading group about horses and take anyone interested in horses? . . . You can't do skill groups if they don't have diversity by class and race. You can't say, 'It's fate,' or 'It's beyond my control because this is the situation.' You have to say, 'Well, it's going to make it harder, now what else can I do?'

Clothing

Another class issue that comes up repeatedly for both Judy and Alma is clothing, an issue from which two important points emerge. First is the need to approach students without fixed preconceptions and assumptions. The other is to refrain from making value judgments; we should observe and try to understand.

Judy talks of middle-class teachers who "sit back from a haughty place and say, 'You ought not to spend your money on Nike sneakers when money is scarce and you should spread it out. You could get a whole outfit for this price'." She also points out how teachers relate differently to poor students who are particularly well dressed versus those who are poorly dressed.

Alma also comments on clothing:

I find that some of my children who are coming from welfare homes, they're dressing, they're bringing in toys, they're sharing things, they're talking about places they go as well as kids who are coming from middle-class homes. Sometimes they have a lot more because a lot of the young, single-family welfare homes put more emphasis on dressing and making sure they're keeping up with, say, Ninja turtles more so than, say, a middle-class home.

Alma has found this situation to be true for the 20 years she has been at her school. Judy also reports that the working-class and poor children tend to be consistently well dressed. She believes middle-class parents are more able to say, "Hey, they're gonna get dirty!" when their kids go off to school. A middle-class teacher may not be too concerned about a child getting paint on his or her clothes, but this can be, in fact, a big deal to a family that has struggled hard to buy those clothes. She finds that families will not send children back to school in those clothes if they cannot get the paint stains out.

The parent wouldn't say you got it in school, you're going back with it to school. That's one of the places where I think we set kids up. We set kids up who are not middle-class kids. We say, 'It's okay if you get paint on yourself.' Well, it's not always okay and that's a place where teachers have to be mindful and not to devalue clothes. The parents work very hard to dress their children and have them ready for school and we can't turn around and say it's okay. So you make sure you either have classroom painting clothes for *everyone* or you have smocks from wrist to knee for everyone. It's important not to sit back and make casual calls.

While quality of clothing may not be as simplistically based on class as we may have thought, economic issues do affect what children have. While many students bring in their own snack, both Alma and Judy serve a "common snack" in their classrooms. They provide an appealing, reasonably nutritious snack (but not so nutritious that it stands out as being different from what the children bring), that is available to everyone and that they themselves eat. In both classrooms, this practice is accepted and enjoyed by the children and brings about a kind of equality during that portion of the children's day.

The Standard Curriculum

Reading plays a crucial role in the interconnection between social class and school achievement. Judy believes that having books at home is directly related to class, not race. She talks of both white kids and black kids from homes where parents are not readers. Judy asks, "How do you encourage more reading at homes that don't do it, without implying that not doing so means there is something wrong with the family?"

For Judy this concern is bound up in her belief that it is absolutely crucial to actively affirm the culture of her students. Many of her Haitian students come from homes where families do not read but where there is a rich storytelling tradition. This is also true for some of the white families in her school where parents are only beginning readers themselves but come from regions of the United States where storytelling is an integral part of the culture. She says that it is important to place a great deal of value on storytelling, acknowledging that passing on stories orally is also a literary tradition. "You give both validity and honor to another kind of literacy. You broaden your sense of literacy to include the verbal piece as well as the written piece." She wants her middle-class students to realize that alternative practices have equal status. "Having a mother who isn't a reader isn't viewed as deficient.

The fact that she isn't a reader isn't what's highlighted. The fact that she is a good storyteller is really important."

Alma provides her own classroom lending library. She says all her students have books at home, but not necessarily the books middle-class teachers expect. The parents of children in her class buy books at the grocery store; they buy coloring books. Alma gives every child a gift of two books each year. In addition, the school has a "home reading program" in which children who read each night for eight weeks get a free book to keep.

School Success

Both Alma and Judy are clear that achievement in their classes, as defined by standardized tests and other commonly used methods, correlates directly with the socioeconomic class of the students. Alma sees that what appears to be standardized scores in Boston based on race are actually ones based on class and are due to the demographics of Boston public schools where middle class and white are highly correlated.

Reflecting on the Boston public schools today, Alma believes teachers often expect less of children from low-income homes. She says that by expecting "utopia" for her children, she makes a major contribution toward their success.

Alma reflects on her own background in order to explain her own understanding of class issues and her teaching style relative to class. Alma grew up in a rural Florida town of 1,500 people with an African American population of 500. Her mother completed 6th grade and her father completed 8th. Alma credits her own educational and professional success and that of her classmates to the support they received growing up. Her teachers were all African American professionals at an all-Black school. They were also all active church members. The students from her small elementary school had to be bused 30 miles to the Black high school. Community expectations were that these students would graduate from college. Although all these children came from homes with parents who had not attended high school, their children did, indeed, *all* graduate from college and many from graduate school. The community provided ongoing support by giving students needed money, clothing and equipment, and sending care packages and checking on grades. "You had a feeling that if you didn't succeed you failed the whole town. We knew that the teachers liked us and wanted us to succeed." Alma sees role models and supportive teachers, parents and community members as central to students' academic achievement.

Both Alma and Judy facilitate parental contact in a variety of ways. This includes phoning and visiting parents at home, showing support for them with their own problems—even those not connected with parenting—and being understanding. They try to be firm and clear about parental responsibilities and provide help when needed. Keeping in mind that some parents do not have the resources or cultural knowledge that will strengthen their children's chances for school success, Alma and Judy share information with parents that will enhance their children's educational opportunities. Some parents, particularly low-income parents, have jobs that do not allow any free time during the day to come to school. Judy and Alma are careful to schedule parent conferences at times convenient to different families.

Alma feels that her school does well in terms of making all children feel welcome and competent. They begin each school year with an emphasis on self-esteem for all children. She says that her 1st- and 2nd-grade children's aspirations are not based on class or race. When she does an activity about "What I Want To Be When I Grow Up," she finds that their goals do not at all correlate with class or race. She also makes a point of presenting children with a range of role models, varied by race and class but with an emphasis away from just white, middle-class role models. Even though most of her African American students come from low-income families, she is able to find parents and friends of their parents who model a range of alternatives. She brings into her classroom guest speakers in a variety of occupations and from a variety of backgrounds.

Judy discusses how values of competition versus cooperation have a major impact. She says the Haitian children talk of "we" not "I." In classroom discussions in Judy's room, the custom is that after a child has finished talking he or she calls on another child rather than having the discussion refocus on Judy. This power sharing has a great effect on the flow of these talks. In the computer lab, the middle-class students tend to talk only with each other in order to compare what lessons they are doing. The Haitian students, on the other hand, are concerned with cooperating and helping each other, even if it means not "getting as far." Judy notes,

We need to really look again at what we value in school. You know we give lip service to cooperation but when kids do it naturally it's counterproductive to what we want when we want them to get this much done in this much time.

Judy believes that this cultural bias towards cooperation can be used to break the "who's at the top" dynamic. Such an effort requires serious restructuring of our classrooms, yet it means important growth in social and academic learning for all children.

You set up situations where there's different leadership. . . .You look at the leadership of kids who are not middle class and say to yourself, 'Let's incorporate that leadership style in our classroom as well.' So 'who's on top' is not always the same.

WHERE DO WE GO FROM HERE?

As we become more aware of and concerned about class issues in our classrooms, we must modify our teaching in many ways. We can develop activities that increase students' awareness of class issues, create new methods for sharing resources within the classroom community, structure reading groups differently, create more inclusive word problems in mathematics and work toward parent involvement programs that respect all parents' skills and needs. In any case, we must reflect on the impact of our actions and classroom culture on children of different socioeconomic classes. In this context, it is important to be conscious of classism in society and how that affects our efforts. For example, since schools are typically funded through property taxes, disproportionately greater resources are available to schools in wealthier communities. While we are working to help students understand and change class bias, they can be simultaneously getting counter-messages condoning classism from other sources, such as television, the neighborhood or family.

For many, all of this discussion may well lead to further questions and concerns. What are some ways that classism cannot be changed merely by what we do at school? What is our role in working on those larger societal changes? What are we doing in our personal lives that reinforces classism? What are we doing to actively work towards change?

RESOURCES
Books for Students (P) - Primary; (E) - Upper Elementary; (M) - Middle School

Bledsoe, L. J. (1995). *The big bike race.* New York: Holiday House. (P)
Brisson, P. (1994). *Wanda's roses.* Honesdale, NY: Boyds Mill Press. (P)
Bunting, E. (1991). *Fly away home.* New York: Clarion Books. (E)
Bunting, E. (1995). *Smoky night.* San Diego: Harcourt Brace Jovanovich. (P)
Byars, B. (1977). *Pinballs.* New York: Harper and Row. (E)
Crutcher, C. (1993). *Staying fat for Sarah Byrnes.* New York: Greenwillow.
Delton, J. (1980). *My mother lost her job today.* Chicago: Whitman. (P)
DiSalvo-Ryan, D. (1991). *Uncle Willie and the soup kitchen.* New York: Morrow Junior Books. (P, E)
Estes, E. (1944). *The hundred dresses.* New York: Harcourt Brace Jovanovich. (M)
Getz, A. (1991). *Tar beach.* New York: Dial Books. (P)
Greenfield, E. (1980). *Grandmama's joy.* New York: Philomel Books. (P)
Hakim, J. (1994). *A history of US.* New York: Oxford University Press. (M)

Hamilton, V. (1986). *The planet of Junior Brown*. New York: MacMillan. (M)

Hansen, J. (1980). *The gift giver*. New York: Clarion. (M)

Hazen, B. S. (1983). *Tight times*. New York: Puffin Books. (P)

Hopkins, L. B. (1992). *Mama*. New York: Simon and Schuster for Young Readers. (E)

Jordan, J. (1975). *New life: New room*. New York: Crowell. (P)

Keats, E. J. (1969). *Goggles*. New York: Collier Books. (P) (and many others by this author)

Kingsolver, B. (1988). *The bean trees*. New York: Harper Row. (M)

Levine, A. (1993). *Pearl Moskowitz's last stand*. New York: Tambourine Books. (P)

Mazer, N. F. (1981). *Mrs. Fish, Ape, and me, the dump queen*. New York: Avon. (M)

McKissack, P. C. & McKissak, F. (1994). *Christmas in the big house, Christmas in the quarters*. New York: Scholastic. (E)

McPherson, S. (1993). *Peace and bread: The story of Jane Addams*. Minneapolis, MN: Carolrhoda. (E)

Miklowitz, G. (1985). *The war between the classes*. New York: Bantam Doubleday. (M)

Mills, L. (1991). *The rag coat*. Boston: Little, Brown and Company. (E)

Mohr, N. (1989). *El Bronx remembered*. Houston: Arte Publico Press. (E) (and others by this author)

Myers, W. D. (1989). *The young landlords*. New York: Puffin Books. (E) (and others by this author)

Patterson, K. (1978). *The great Gilly Hopkins*. New York: Crowell. (E)

Radin, R. (1991). *All Joseph wanted*. New York: MacMillan. (E)

Sachs, M. (1971). *The bear's house*. Garden City, NY: Doubleday. (U) (and others by this author)

Seifer, N. (Ed.) (1976). *Nobody speaks for me! Self portraits of working class women*. New York: Simon and Schuster. (E)

Soto, G. (1993). *The pool party*. New York: Dell Books. (E)

Taylor, B. (1994). *The table where rich people sit*. New York: Charles Scribner's Sons Books for Young Readers. (E)

Taylor, M. (1976). *Roll of thunder, hear my cry*. New York: Dial Press. (E) (and others by this author)

Thomas, L. (1979). *Hi, Mrs. Mallory!* New York: Harper and Row, Inc. (P)

Voight, C. (1981). *Homecoming*. New York: Fawcett, Jr. (E) (and others in this series)

Williams, V. (1993). *Scooter*. New York: Greenwillow.

Williams, V. B. (1982). *A chair for my mother*. New York: Greenwillow. (P) (and others in this series)

Wolff, V. (1993). *Make lemonade*. New York: Henry, Holt and Co. (M)

Woodson, J. (1992). *Last summer with Maizon*. New York: Dell Publishing. (E) (and others in this series)

Woodson, J. (1994). *I didn't mean to tell you this*. New York: Delacorte. (M) (and others by this author)

Resources for Teachers

Amott, T., & Matthei, J. (1991). *Race, gender and work: A multicultural economic history of women in the United States*. Boston: South End Press.

Arnow, H. (1954). *The dollmaker*. New York: Avon.

Barlett, D., & Steele, J. (1992). *America: What went wrong?* Kansas City, MO: Andrews and McMeel Publishers.

Barlett, D., & Steele, J. (1994). *America: Who really pays taxes*. New York: Simon and Schuster.

Baxandall, R. (1995). *America's working women: A documentary history*. New York: Vintage.

Brouwer, S. (1992). *Sharing the pie: A disturbing picture of the U.S. economy*. Carlisle, PA: Big Picture Books.

Coalition for Basic Needs. (1990). *Up and out of poverty campaign*. Cambridge, MA: Author. (Updated Yearly).

Cose, E. (1993). *The rage of the privileged class*. New York: Harper Collins.

Dollars and sense. (n.d.). 1 Summer Street, Somerville, MA 02143.

deLone, R., & Carnegie Council on Children. (1979). *Small futures: Children, inequality and the limits of liberal reform*. New York: Harcourt, Brace Jovanovich.

Dixon, B. (1977). *Catching them young: Sex, race and class in children's fiction*. London: Pluto Press.

Dorsey-Gaines, C., & Taylor, D. (1988). *Growing up literate: Learning from inner city families*. Portsmouth, NH: Hienemann.

Folbre, N., & Center for Popular Economics. (1995). *The new field guide to the U.S. economy*. New York: New Press.

Frazier, T. (1974). *The underside of American history*. New York: Harcourt, Brace, Jovanovich.

Kowalski, L. (Director). (1991). *Rock soup*. [video]. New York: First Run/Icarus Films.

Kotlowitz, A. (1991). *There are no children here: The story of two boys growing up in the other America*. New York: Anchor Books.

Lukas, J. A. (1986). *Common ground*. New York: Vintage.

Matthews, J. (1988). *Escalante: The best teacher in America*. New York: Henry Holt and Co.

Nieto, S. (1995). *Affirming diversity: The sociopolitical context of multicultural education*. New York: Longman.

Parenti, M. (1994). *Democracy for the few*. New York: St. Martins Press.

Pizzigati, S. (1992). *The maximum wage: A common sense prescription for revitalizing America by taxing the very rich*. Apex Press.

Randy, A., & Center for Popular Economics. (1988). *Mink coats don't trickle down*. Boston: South End Press.

Rose, S. (1992). *Social stratification in the United States*. New York: New Press.

Rubin, L. B. (1976). *Worlds of pain: Life in the working class family*. New York: Basic Books.

Ryan, W. (1976). *Blaming the victim*. New York: Vintage Press.

Ryan, W. (1982). *Equality*. New York: Pantheon.

Schniedewind, N., & Davidson, E. (1983, 2nd edition in press 1996). *Open minds to equality: Learning activities to promote race, sex, class and age equity*. Englewood Cliffs, NJ: Prentice-Hall.

Schniedewind, N., & Davidson, E. (1987). *Cooperative learning, cooperative lives: A sourcebook of learning activities for building a peaceful new world*. Dubuque, Iowa: W.C. Brown.

Sennett, R., & Cobb, J. (1993). *The hidden injuries of class*. New York: Vintage.

Shange, N. (1985). *Betsey Brown*. New York: St. Martins Press.

Sidel, R. (1983). *Women and children last*. New York: Viking Books.

Sklar, H. (1995). *Chaos or community: Seeking solutions, not scapegoats for bad economics*. Boston: South End Press.

Sleeter, C., & Grant, C. (1994). *Making choices for multicultural education: Five approaches to race, class, and gender*. New York: MacMillan.

Smedley, A. (1973). *Daughter of the earth*. Old Westbury, NY: Feminist Press.

Yates, P. (Director). (1987). *Four voices*. [video]. New York: First Run/Icarus Films.

References

Anyon, J. (1981). Social class and the hidden curriculum of work. In H. Giroux, A. Penna & W. F. Pinar (Eds.), *Curriculum and instruction* (pp. 317-341). Berkeley, CA: McCutcheon.

Bellenca, J., & Schwartz, E. (1993). *The challenge of detracking*. New York: Skylight Publications.

Delpit, L. (1995). *Other people's children: Cultural conflict in the classroom*. New York: New Press.

Hacker, A. (1992). *Two nations: Black and white, separate, hostile, unequal*. New York: Scribners.

Jencks, C. (1979). *Who gets ahead?* New York: Basic Books.

Kozol, J. (1991). *Savage inequalities: Children in America's schools*. New York: HarperCollins.

Lerner, G. (1973). *The black woman in white America: A documentary history*. New York: Vintage Books.

Lortie, D. (1975). *Schoolteacher: A sociological study*. Chicago, IL: Chicago Press.

Oakes, J. (1986). *Keeping track: How schools structure inequality*. New Haven: Yale University Press.

Rist, R. (1970). Student social class and teacher expectations: The self-fulfilling prophecy in ghetto education. *Harvard Educational Review, 40*(3), 411-450.

Sanders, B. (1994, January 16). Whither American democracy. *Los Angeles Times*, p. A2.

Schniedewind, N., & Davidson, E. (1987). *Cooperative learning, cooperative lives: A sourcebook of learning activities for building a peaceful new world*. Dubuque, IA: W. C. Brown.

Willie, C. (1985). *Black and white families: A study in complementarity*. Bayside, NY: General Hall.

Wilson, W. J. (1996). *When work disappears: The world of the new urban poor*. New York: Knopf.

Zinn, H. (1980). *A people's history of the United States*. New York: Harper, Row.

Acknowledgments:

The authors would like to thank Judy Richards and Alma Wright for sharing their experiences as teachers; Jim Hammerman and Laurie Prendergast for insightful discussions throughout the writing of this chapter; and Savanna Books in Cambridge, Massachusettes, and Odyssey Books in South Hadley, Massachusettes, for help with the bibliography.

Chapter 5

Language Diversity in the Classrooms

Deborah A. Byrnes and Diana Cortez

According to the 1990 U.S. census, approximately one in seven U.S. residents speaks a language other than English at home (National Education Association, 1993). The number of school-age children who speak English as a second language is estimated to be between 3.5 to 5.5 million students, depending upon the method used for identification (Garcia, 1996, p. 802). These children, many of them immigrants, represent linguistic and cultural groups as diverse as Haitians, Afghanis, Hmongs and Tongans. Unfortunately, most teachers have little experience or training to work with linguistically diverse children and, consequently, experts estimate that over two-thirds of these children are not receiving appropriate instruction (Soto, 1991; Waggoner & O'Malley, 1985). In addition, growing public support for language-protectionist groups (e.g., the English-only movement) suggests that many language-minority children may experience openly negative attitudes toward their home language (Daniels, 1990).

With more and more linguistically diverse children entering classrooms, teachers must address language diversity as part of cultural diversity within the classroom. They must examine their own attitudes and the attitudes of their students toward speakers of other languages (Adler, 1993). When a teacher and student can communicate through a common language, they have a greater ability to share their cultures and learn from one another. When the child does not speak English and the teacher does not speak the child's language, both culture and language limit communication. Teachers often feel frustrated because they have no way of understanding the child's culture, what the child knows, how they feel or what they need in the way of instruction. Frustration can turn into anger as teachers realize they are accountable for teaching this child, without the training or resources for doing so.

This chapter examines issues related to language differences confronting the regular classroom teacher who has linguistically diverse children in his or her classroom for some part of the day. The authors begin by reviewing several important background points that classroom teachers need to be aware of if they are to be more sensitive to the needs and experiences of linguistic minorities. They also make specific suggestions for teaching linguistically diverse students and address how teachers can help English-only students to be sensitive to language differences. The chapter concludes with a short case study of one classroom teacher's work with language-minority students, including suggested resources and references for classroom teachers.

UNDERSTANDING LANGUAGE DIFFERENCES AND LANGUAGE LEARNING

A number of important points and misconceptions regarding linguistic differences and second-language learning need to be addressed before discussing specific strategies for working with linguistic minorities. The following section introduces some basic concepts and issues relevant to language diversity.

Language and Culture Are Inseparable

An intimate relationship exists between language and culture. Through socialization into our culture, we acquire language. Language, in turn, shapes our perception of the physical world around us, the social world in which we live and the spiritual (or metaphysical) world that gives meaning to our lives (see Farb, 1975, for a discussion on the "Sapir-Whorf hypothesis"; that is, the notion that language shapes our view of reality). In many Asian languages, for example, words or word markers indicate the social status of the speaker and the person being addressed. These words denote a person's relative position in the social order and the rights (e.g., commanding respect and reverence) and obligations (e.g., showing deference) he or she has compared to others.

Some languages, like English and Hopi, come from radically different cultures. Embedded in the languages are two totally different perceptions of reality (Hall, 1973). The Hopi language, for example, has no nouns and no verb tenses. If one wanted to refer to a table, the rough translation into English would be "tabling"—the table has always existed in a spiritual sense, it exists now and will exist forever. The metaphysical or spiritual view implied by the Hopi language is one in which time is not linear—a view that is difficult, if not impossible, for English speakers to grasp. Language, then, serves "both as a conveyor of culture and as an extension and expression of culture" (Newmark & Asante, 1976, p. 4).

Consequently, one cannot effectively address linguistic differences without acknowledging and respecting cultural differences. Conversely, one cannot respect cultural differences without acknowledging and understanding the importance of a person's language. A child thinks and understands the world in his or her language. Language is intricately tied to a child's identity. Ignoring or devaluing the child's native language is denying an important part of who the child is and the rich store of past and present cultural experiences the child brings to school. Thus, it is critical for a classroom teacher to acknowledge and respect a child's home language, whether it is a completely different language or a variant of English, such as African American or Appalachian English.

Bilingual/Bicultural Children

A teacher's goal should be to help language-minority children become bilingual so they can have access to two cultures. Unfortunately, many children, when we try to teach them English, lose their primary language (Wong-Fillmore, 1990). Children living in the United States learn that English is the primary language of education, business, mass media and government. English is associated with success and high status. In an effort to be part of this new, successful and high-status community, and not to stand out or be different, children may give up speaking their native language. Teachers may consciously or unconsciously foster this rejection by not demonstrating respect for a child's language and culture and by encouraging a child to speak English even while at home (Wong-Fillmore, 1990; Wong-Fillmore & Valadez, 1986).

This move away from speaking one's native language may have unanticipated consequences for home life. If a child's parents are not proficient in English and the child begins speaking English at home, communication between child and parents often erodes. Parents lose their ability to communicate important values to their children and to pass on important cultural traditions and lessons. Family unity and closeness may be sacrificed when children adopt English as their primary language. Instead of encouraging parents and children to practice English at home, teachers should support parents in helping their children become more proficient speakers of their native language.

Ironically, the advantages of speaking a second language are touted by educators across the nation (e.g., Willis, 1996), yet the second-language resources brought to school by many language-minority children are ignored. Advocates of foreign-language study admonish schools to put more emphasis on teaching foreign languages, yet immigrant children are rapidly mainstreamed in such a way that many of them lose their mother tongue and later qualify for foreign-language instruction in their native language (Wyner, 1989). Maintaining and developing students' home languages is an obvious way to enhance individuals' development, helping them to become bilingual/bicultural, while also helping to overcome foreign-language incompetence in the United States.

Language-Minority Students: A Diverse Group
Children who do not speak English or have limited knowledge of English are incredibly diverse and have a wide range of educational needs. Some of the diverse groups included under the label of language-minority students, according to Myer (1985), are: 1) Immigrant children educated in their native language but with little or no exposure to English. They need assistance with English and with understanding the new culture in which they are now living. 2) Immigrant children with little or no exposure to English and, due to political or economic turmoil, little or no education in their native language. These children need instruction in basic educational concepts as well as English and American culture. 3) Immigrant children who have learned some English in their previous countries but are not familiar with American culture. Such children have a head start but will still need assistance with the language and culture. 4) U.S.-born children in nonEnglish-speaking homes. These children may know little English but have the advantage of being familiar with the culture.

Stages in Learning a Second Language
Within each of the above groups, children will be at different stages of learning English (Myer, 1985). When children are first introduced to a new language community, they generally listen actively and try to make sense of the language. They will say little or nothing. Children begin to understand simple and familiar English long before they are ready or able to verbalize for themselves in the new language. As children become more familiar with the language, they will begin imitating simple phrases and statements in context. As they gain experience and confidence, they will go beyond imitating and will begin to experiment with the language. Language is now used to create new communications. Many errors in grammar and pronunciation are made at this stage. Eventually, children internalize most of the rules and can use more complex structures and make fewer errors. Children are now able to express complex ideas in their new language. At each stage, teachers need to be supportive and provide lessons and activities that are appropriate for the child's stage of language learning.

Learning a Language Takes Time
Learning a language is a gradual process. Some research suggests that words must be heard over 200 times before they become part of a learner's repertoire. Competence in informal communication in social settings, often referred to as basic interpersonal communication skills (BICS), may develop in one to two years. In contrast, it generally takes five to seven years to achieve cognitive academic language proficiency (CALP), which is the type of language knowledge needed for formal and context-reduced environments (Cheng, 1987; Kottler, 1994). Because new concepts and abstract ideas are constantly being introduced in school, language-minority children do not fully benefit from their schooling until achieving CALP. Because informal, context-embedded language is acquired first and most rapidly, teachers should be careful not to assume language-minority children know more English than they actually do. A child who appears to be quite fluent in English on the playground, may still be unable to comprehend a classroom lecture on the Civil War unless accompanied by many extralinguistic cues.

Language learning takes as long, if not longer, for younger children. It is often believed that young children learn a second language more easily and more quickly than older children or adults. Research evidence, however, does not support this belief (Collier, 1987). The only aspect of language learning in which younger children seem to do better is the development of a more native-like accent and pronunciation (Soto, 1991).

Attitudes and Motivation Are Important

Language learning is greater when children have positive attitudes about the language and are motivated to learn it. Most children learn English without making a conscious decision to do so. Children learn a second language because it meets their needs. They learn English so they can interact with friends, learn interesting and relevant information, read for pleasure and understand movies and songs.

A teacher's warmth and interest in the language-monority child will influence the student's attitudes about school, English speakers and the English language. The teacher's words and actions must convey respect for the child's language and culture. Children must also sense that the teacher has faith in their ability to learn and believes they are worthwhile persons (Kottler, 1994). A child who feels valued and self-confident is more likely to be a successful second-language learner.

Language Diversity in America

The United States has a long history of language diversity. We tend to forget that language was an issue for all immigrants to America, except those from the British Isles. The vast majority of native English-speaking individuals in the United States are descendents of Americans who came to the country speaking a language other than English. Historically, a typical family required four generations to move from being monolingual in a nonEnglish language to being monolingual in English (Valdes, 1990). First-generation immigrants principally spoke their native language. Their facility with English was likely minimal or nonexistent. (In the late 1700s, Western European groups, such as the French, Dutch and Germans, set up their own schools using the language of the largest group as the language of instruction [Williams, 1991].) The second generation spoke some English but still used their parents' language primarily. Third-generation Americans used English primarily, and possessed only limited fluency in their grandparents' language. Fourth-generation Americans often spoke only English. With such a progression, it was not unusual for children to be unable to communicate with their great-grandparents.

When native English speakers resent the time it takes to communicate with persons limited in their knowledge of English or suggest that immigrants should learn English or leave, they might do well to consider their own ancestors. Learning a new language and culture takes time. Many native English speakers do not need to look back very many generations to find family members who were themselves limited in their English proficiency.

TEACHING LANGUAGE-MINORITY CHILDREN IN THE REGULAR CLASSROOM

If we were to consider pedagogical effectiveness and instructional efficiency, children would be taught content in their native language (Williams, 1991) and English would be taught as a second language. It only makes sense that children will learn skills and content more quickly and more easily in the language they know best. How much would we would learn if asked to attend an important education lecture given in a language we did not understand well? It takes years for children to become fluent in a new language. Consequently, they miss much of content that is being taught.

Unfortunately, many political and economic reasons mean that bilingual or English-As-a-Second-Language classrooms are unavailable to many language-minority students (e.g., Ruiz, 1991; Willis, 1994). Thus, the responsibility of doing the best to help language-minority children retain their home language, and learn English and subject content at the same time, falls upon the regular, classroom teacher who is likely to speak only English. Here are some useful ideas for providing the best possible instruction under the above circumstances.

Teaching Style

Evidence suggests that specific styles of teaching can influence the amount of English a language-minority student will learn and, consequently, the amount of content the student learns. The following suggestions, synthesized from the work of Gersten (1996), Kottler (1994), Wong-Fillmore (1985, 1989), and Wong-Fillmore and Valadez (1986), can help the regular-classroom teacher work more effectively with language-minority students while teaching the usual subject matter.

Focused lessons. Effective teachers of linguistically diverse students examine the content of the material they are teaching and directly focus students on the critical vocabulary and concepts necessary for understanding new ideas. They do not assume that students understand such words as "globe," "inventor" or "suspicious." The teacher plans many opportunities for the students to apply new concepts and vocabulary in interactions with teacher and peers. Most important, they engage students in dialogues that require higher-level thinking. For example, if a child states that a character in a book was suspicious, other students may be asked to provide evidence of the character's "suspicious" behavior. A teacher-directed lesson may work well here because the teacher can ensure that all children have a good language model and that all children reach an adequate level of concept development. In contrast, individualized classrooms with individual work assignments do not appear to foster language development because the amount of language practice a child gets depends on individual circumstances. Shy or unassertive children may have little opportunity to interact in English in such a classroom.

Patterns and routines. Children in classrooms with teachers who follow distinct patterns day after day, who have established routines and consistency in organization, learn more English than students in less-structured classrooms. In classrooms with patterns and routines, children do not have to figure out what is going on every day. They can concentrate on the language and what they are supposed to be learning.

Student participation. The presence of structured ways in which students participate also helps students learn English. A teacher might first ask for volunteers, then request group responses and finally establish turn-taking that requires every student to contribute. Of course, questions directed to language-minority students should be geared to their language abilities. Unfortunately, in many classrooms children who know the language are given more practice and feedback than children who are learning English. This is particularly true in classroom where only volunteers (i.e., the most assertive students) participate.

Presentation style. Language-minority students learn more English when the teacher takes special care to speak clearly and use concrete references, repetitions, rephrasings, gestures, visual aides and demonstrations. It is important to remember that the child who does not receive instruction in his or her native language is totally dependent on the teacher's ability to make communication meaningful.

The teaching strategies described above may not be the best examples of creative teaching. They do, however, appear to help language-monority students be more successful at language learning.

Appropriate Content

Children need content that is on an appropriate cognitive level. Giving a kindergarten workbook to a language-minority 4th-grader who was performing at grade level before coming to the United States is not appropriate. To learn a second language, children need to be interested in learning it. Students are often embarrassed by and uninterested in materials far below their grade level. Consequently, they may lose interest in school and learning English. Inappropriate materials can also lead to permanent tracking in lower levels. Whenever possible, content and supporting activities (adapted for the linguistically diverse child) should be drawn from grade-level curriculum.

For the child who is intrigued by computers, teachers may want to consider some of the new multimedia programs that have been developed to help children learn English (Allen, 1996). *The Rosetta Stone*, by Fairfield Language Technologies, includes English-language skill building on themes such as food, houses, clothes and communication. It is designed for grades 3 and up. Another program, DynED's *Let's Go*, is an interactive CD-ROM designed for children ages 4-10. Lessons on weather, parts of the body, colors and household objects can be used to reinforce English vocabulary in an enjoyable and novel manner. Many of the new child-friendly word-processing programs are also a real asset to English-language learners because they allow students to focus on meaning while receiving assistance with vocabulary, spelling and grammar.

Realistic Expectations
Teachers should ask themselves, "If I did not understand English, would I be able to get some meaning from what is occurring in the classroom?" Make it possible, through the use of extralinguistic cues, for the language-minority child to get something out of every lesson. It is important to recognize that language-minority students will not get everything that is in the curriculum at the level appropriate for native English speakers. Realistic expectations with respect to language learning and understanding of content are critical.

Native Language Support Materials
Instruction in a child's native language is necessary to provide full access to the content areas. Support materials in the native language should be used as instructional tools for both language acquisition and content area instruction. Paraprofessionals and other community resources may have appropriate resources. Some libraries, refugee centers and cultural centers have books that may be of help to nonEnglish-speaking students who are literate in their home languages. Distributors of children's books and dictionaries in foreign languages also have excellent materials (check with your local bookstore). Text-book publishers may have foreign-language editions of their textbooks. A parent or volunteer who speaks the child's language can also be recruited to read to the child in the native language and tutor when appropriate.

Learn About the Culture and Language
Teachers should become familiar with the languages and cultures of the students they teach, recognizing and respecting cultural differences. By learning about various cultural and linguistic differences, the teacher can be more responsive to the child's emotional and instructional needs. For example, some Native American children may consider a teacher's normal teaching voice to be loud, indicating anger or meanness (Grove, 1976). Children from some cultures may have been taught that it is inappropriate to volunteer information. Knowledge of values and beliefs, such as concepts of kinship, family patterns and appropriate social proximity, are particularly necessary in order to communicate effectively with family members.

A teacher who learns to speak some of the child's language, even if only a few words and phrases, can enhance the child's self-image and help other students recognize that the teacher values and appreciates other languages (Perez, 1979). If the teacher makes mistakes, the child also has the satisfaction of helping the teacher and being in the role of the expert.

Effective Teaching Strategies That Benefit All Children

Several general teaching strategies currently being implemented in many elementary schools can be especially helpful for English-language learners. Cooperative-learning groups and peer or cross-age tutoring can benefit all children (Cazden, 1988; Kottler, 1994). With an English-language learner, it is important to examine your learning objective before deciding in which group or team to place the child. Generally, heterogeneous groups are recommended. If a child knows little or no English and the content is very important, however, placing the child with a bilingual child would be a real advantage. It might be appropriate to place children who speak the same foreign language in a group together with a bilingual volunteer, if available. This should only be done when content learning is more important than the acquisition of English. If language learning is considered to be more important, the language-minority child should be placed with compassionate and competent speakers of English (Wong-Fillmore, 1989).

Many instructional strategies emerging from the whole-language movement are also beneficial for English-language learners (Abramson, Seda & Johnson, 1990; Hudelson, 1986). Whole-language classrooms provide many opportunities for rich, meaningful interactions with language. Children are encouraged to view learning about language, both oral and written, as natural and exciting. They are allowed to work at their own levels and to support one another in their individual efforts. Print-rich environments that include daily journal writing are great for children who are learning a new language. Predictable books that help children learn about structural regularities of the language are also highly recommended (Hough, Nurss & Enright, 1986; Moustafa, 1980).

TEACHING CHILDREN ABOUT LANGUAGE DIFFERENCES

A child from a nonEnglish-language background may feel isolated not only because of the inability to communicate with others, but also because other students see the student as different and inferior and thus may avoid, tease or exclude the child. How one speaks and what language someone speaks immediately evokes certain attitudinal reactions in the listener (Adler, 1993; Gardner & Lambert, 1972). Individuals associate certain ways of talking with particular persons who use that language, often affected by social and racial attitudes. Attitudes children form about language differences may be based on personal experiences, or a child may have learned such attitudes indirectly from hearing or observing the responses of other people. Some languages and accents have greater stigmatizing power than others.

Teachers must work to eliminate stereotypes and misconceptions children may hold regarding speakers of other languages or speakers of nonstandard varieties of English. Children must learn that no language or dialect is intrinsically good or bad, correct or incorrect. All languages are tools for communicating ideas within a given speech community (Taylor, 1986; Tiedt & Tiedt, 1990).

Activities To Build Understanding of Language Differences

Learning about languages and language differences is one way children can gain insights into culture and increase their understanding and acceptance of cultural and linguistic minorities. Here are some possible activities:

■ Have a person who speaks another language give a lesson and assignment to the class in a foreign language. Afterward, have the children share their feelings. Discuss how nonEnglish-speaking people may feel when they do not understand much of what is going on around them. Help the children understand that people generally do not give much thought to language unless put in a position where they cannot understand what someone is saying. You may want to compare it to oxygen. Nobody focuses on the critical need for oxygen until put into a situation where it is lacking. Have the children discuss how they can help learners of English as a second language in their own communities.

■ International movies can also provide sensitizing experiences. Most large video stores carry subtitled international movies in many different languages that can be shown to elicit discussion on languages. Preview the movie before using it as a teaching tool to ensure that segments shown are acceptable for children and do not create negative attitudes toward the language group. Because older children will likely read the subtitles, the teacher may want to hold a narrow piece of poster board over the subtitles. Students can discuss what they think was being said and how it feels not to understand a language. This activity can also be used to examine nonverbal behavior in other cultures.

■ Help students understand how languages differ and how challenging it is to learn a new language by providing an opportunity for them to learn a new language. If the children can learn at least a little of another child's language, communication between the class and the child may be enhanced. Additionally, the learner of English senses that he or she has something important to share.

■ Children usually recognize that individuals from different cultures may have different clothing, housing and language. Generally, however, they do not understand that a language and culture may reflect ideas and concepts that do not exist in or are quite different from their own culture (Welton, 1990). Children, and adults, often have difficulty understanding that others may look at the world quite differently. Most children believe that one can translate one language directly into another without any loss of meaning.

Ask a bilingual person to talk to the class about how they deal with two languages. Children may not realize that a simple statement such as "I miss you" would be constructed differently in another language. In French, for example, the literal translation would be, "You are lacking to me." English statements such as "I'll be darned" may have no direct translation in another language. The translator must search for a replacement that conveys a similar meaning in the other culture. Even words having direct counterparts in another language may have slightly different meanings. The word "sharp" in English can have a positive connotation, such as a "sharp" thinker or "sharp" dresser. In Chinese, however, sharp connotes cunning and is considered a negative term. Children may be interested to learn that even speakers of the same language may interpret words differently. In Ireland you would ask for a "lift to the store" never a "ride to the store." A "tonic" on the West Coast of the United States is a medicinal stimulant. On the East Coast it is a soft drink.

■ Children must understand that words alone are not the only means of conveying a message. Sometimes a large part of the message is shared through culturally specific ways of speaking. By using a different tone of voice and different inflection the statement, "It's raining outside," can sound like a question, an exciting event or a depressing fact. Help children understand that tone, pitch, tempo and use of pauses in speech convey meaning. Discuss how a new learner of a language has to learn much more than vocabulary.

How tone, pitch, tempo and pauses are used varies across cultures. Students may find it interesting to know that in many Asian languages words have only one syllable. The same one-syllable word can have many different meanings, depending on pitch or tone (Welton, 1990). For example, the word "nam" in Vietnamese can mean several different things, depending on pitch. The importance of pitch in Asian languages gives them a singsong quality that also influences the written language. Since all the variations in pitch would be difficult to represent when writing the language, many Asian languages use pictographs rather than phonetic symbols.

■ Share books that involve characters being placed in situations where they have to learn another language and culture. Discuss the role of language in the character's life. Help the children develop understanding for what it must be like not to understand what is going on around you. (Examples of such books can be found in the resource section of this chapter, as can a number of interesting children's books that deal directly with language learning and differences.)

■ Explore the linguistic diversity that may exist in your own classroom. What languages are represented in the classrom and in the student's extended families? For those whose families only speak English, have them find out what languages their ancestors spoke. List all the languages and show the countries of origin on a map. Children will quickly realize that most of them have family members (past or present) who have struggled to learn English when they first came to the United States.

■ If any children in the class have traveled in another country where they did not know the language, ask them to share their experience. It is important, however, to realize that English speakers generally have an advantage in world travel. The English language is widely spoken in many countries; English speakers are not likely to feel the same sense of helplessness, confusion and fear that nonEnglish-speaking immigrants to America do.

■ Older children might benefit from lessons on the historical evolution of various languages and dialects, regional differences and similarities and differences among various language systems. Many people do not realize that geographical barriers (e.g, mountains, rivers, lakes) have isolated certain groups of people and led to mild to extreme language differences among peoples that live geographically adjacent to each other.

■ Often, children do not understand why second-language learners sound different than native speakers. They probably are not aware that some sounds they take for granted, such as the "th" sound, do not exist in many other languages. Speakers of English as a second language will replace the unknown sound with one that is familiar. In the case of the "th" it may be replaced with a "zee" or a "d" sound. Children can be helped to understand that we develop a sound system based on the languages we hear as we are learning how to talk. As we grow older, it is more difficult to produce sounds we did not learn as we first learned how to talk. To illustrate your point more effectively, ask the class to try making sounds that other languages use but are not present in the English language. Examples of such sounds are the rolled "r" in Spanish, the nasal vowel sounds in French or the clicks used in some African languages. If you are unable to model the sounds and do not have access to someone you can record, look for language-learning tapes or multimedia.

■ Children should also learn to value various English dialects and accents, recognizing all varieties of English as valid forms of communication and dialects and accents as reflections of cultural and social variations within a broader language group (Taylor, 1986). Children can be exposed to a variety of forms of English through reading various stories aloud or listening to tapes of various dialects. Regional and social dialects from various television programs can be discussed. Throughout such lessons, it is important that the class reflect a positive attitude of respect and enjoyment as they listen to the variety of accents.

CASE STUDY

Julie Becker[1] has made improving education for language-minority children in regular classrooms her professional goal. A classroom teacher in Salt Lake City, Utah, for 12 years, Julie also spent six years as an education specialist and consultant for other teachers who are addressing the needs of culturally and linguistically different children. Julie's focus on linguistic minorities started many years ago when a boy from Mexico joined her 3rd-grade classroom. Miguel did not speak any English. As many teachers do, Julie turned to her school district for support and materials, only to find she was basically on her own. Miguel would get some tutoring in English, but what happened in her own classroom was up to her. She took the challenge of teaching Miguel very seriously and, soon, other language-minority children entering 3rd grade at her school were placed in her classroom.

---

[1]Julie Becker is a teacher in the Granite Public School District in Salt Lake City, Utah. She may be contacted at Truman Elementary, 4639 South 3200 West, Salt Lake City, Utah 84065.

Julie feels it is essential that teachers' attitudes toward receiving nonEnglish-speaking children in their classroom should be one of acceptance, understanding and compassion. If the teacher shows signs of being upset, indifferent or frustrated, the entire class will feel the tension and respond in a negative manner. Julie acknowledges that it is normal to feel frustrated, but stresses that having English language learners in the classroom does not have to be a negative experience.

Creating a loving, caring, supportive and stimulating environment for every student is important to Julie. For such an environment to exist, she believes all students must be engaged in the process. When a new student who does not speak English enters her classroom, she enlists all of her students' help. She begins by helping her students understand what it is like to come to a different country and a new classroom where nothing is familiar and everything is written and spoken in another language. She encourages her students to empathize with the new children by talking to them and writing on the chalkboard in another language. (She suggests making up a language if you do not know one.)

Julie encourages her students to help the child learn English and to make an effort to learn some of the child's language. They are encouraged to include the new student in play at recess. Initially, a buddy is assigned each day to help the new child feel included and to help him or her learn playground and classroom routines. In class, Julie seats the child next to a capable and kind child and for a limited time encourages the new child to copy, as needed, from this student's paper. She is usually pleased by the amount of peer tutoring, albeit nonverbal, that occurs in such situations. She always stresses to the other children that the new student is not cheating and that they would receive the same kind of assistance if they did not speak the language.

Julie always praises her students for being helpful and for teaching positive words and behaviors to English language learners. She finds that if children are not sensitively engaged in helping the new child, they sometimes engage in counterproductive teaching. For example, some students might think it is great fun to teach a child swear words and encourage him or her to act in socially unacceptable ways. She immediately confronts such behavior on the part of English-speaking students.

Whenever a teacher receives a child from another culture, Julie thinks it is essential that the teacher gain some information on the child's culture in order to communicate effectively with both the child and his or her family. When a student from another country joins her class, everyone spends time learning about the country and discussing cultural differences in an accepting and positive manner. Julie cautions, however, that it is important to know what a child's experience was in their country. Some children may come from refugee camps or other experiences that affect them deeply. American students need to understand how such experiences can affect a newcomer's perspective and behavior so that they can be more understanding of their new classmate. At all times, respect and courtesy toward the child's culture should be shown.

Julie helps her language-minority students learn English and function easily in her classroom in many ways. She labels items in her classroom in both English and the child's language and her hall passes have both pictures and words to indicate a child getting a drink of water, going to the restroom or going to English-as-a-Second-Language (ESL) class at a certain time. This way, the child can get his or her basic needs met without embarrassment. She encourages and accepts any attempts the student makes to communicate, recognizing that it might be months before the student feels comfortable speaking in a new language. Julie soon learned the importance of using many visual cues and demonstrations with her class and repeating or paraphrasing important concepts and directions several times.

Julie found that language-minority children can understandably become behavior problems if asked to sit all day in class without understanding what is going on around them and getting little recognition for what they do know. Consequently, she tries to incorporate the child's language into many aspects of the classroom and to challenge native English-speaking students to learn another language. When children were working in cooperative groups, for example, she requires them to ask for and name colors in Spanish. Her Spanish-speaking students become assets to their groups. She also includes bonus spelling words for the whole class in the language of the nonEnglish-speaking student. To help other children feel comfortable engaging the language-minority students in play and other activities, she teaches her class basic verbs (e.g., to play, to help, to eat, to run and to work) in the foreign language. Students often ask her for more words as their desire to communicate in the child's language increases. Even if you do not know the language, foreign-language dictionaries may be enough to provide minimal communication. Asking the child to help with pronunciation is always a good idea.

Where possible, English-language learners are provided textbooks and storybooks to read in their native language. Her district houses a multicultural library that offers Spanish textbooks, foreign-language dictionaries, children's literature in a variety of languages and sheltered-English instruction materials. Julie has found some excellent, sheltered-English textbooks that she incorporates into her social studies curriculum. These books provide content instruction in easier-to-understand language that has controlled vocabulary and idioms. While teachers can design their own sheltered-English materials, more and more published programs are available to assist teachers. Given time constraints, Julie encourages teachers to consider what is already published.

Julie also encourages language-minority children to write stories in their first language, while others write in English. The children then share their stories in class orally just like everyone else. She feels that such efforts communicate to English language learners that she respects their language and that it is important to continue learning in one's home language. Julie believes this practice also helps her English-speaking students develop empathy by getting a sample of what it is like for a nonEnglish-speaking student to listen to an entire lesson delivered in English. These experiences also demonstrate to the rest of the class that she, as the teacher, values different languages.

Julie admits that some language-minority students may not want public attention, particularly if they have been in the United States for a while and have developed the attitude that speaking a language other than English is not prestigious. Such children may feel uncomfortable if they are asked to translate or speak their native language. They do not want to appear different. Obviously, their desire not to use their native language should be respected. Any undue pressure to speak their home language in an English environment will simply add to their discomfort.

Julie considers it important to regularly adjust the curriculum to provide activities that are challenging, but not overwhelming, for language-minority students. For example, learners of the English language are given a shorter set of spelling words to learn; additional words are added gradually as language mastery develops. As mentioned earlier, words in the child's native language are also included and given as bonus words to the entire class.

When adjusting the curriculum, it is important to give up some of the grading expectations teachers may have. Julie encourages teachers to reduce some of the stress they feel evaluating language-minority children by initially grading only in some areas. As the child gains more facility with English, other areas can be added. It is senseless, in her opinion, to feel you must grade learners of the English language on the same scale as native English speakers. Grades based on assignments in a language that a child does not understand are hardly fair assessments and serve only to discourage the child. With a new language-minority student, Julie sometimes grades only in math and handwriting during the first grading session. She sends home a handwritten note with the first report card so that they will understand why she is not grading in all areas. When she cannot get the note translated, she sends it in English. Julie has found that parents usually either have enough English competence to understand the notes or they know someone who can translate for them. Communication in English is better than no communication at all.

Julie also makes an effort to coordinate her work with language-minority students with whatever kind of special instruction they are receiving. She finds that it is often possible to integrate and reinforce the learning that is taking place in those other settings. Taking time to find out what the child is being taught by an ESL teacher or tutor can help create a more consistent and integrated learning environment.

Julie accepts language diversity in her classroom and takes advantage of it. As demonstrated by this short case study, linguistically diverse students do create extra work for the classroom teacher, but they also provide opportunities for the teacher and English-speaking students to grow in their understanding, knowledge and acceptance of language and cultural differences. In turn, language-minority children who have teachers like Julie can learn English and acquire knowledge in a positive and supportive environment that respects their home culture and language.

CONCLUSION

We can do much to help learners of English as a second language function more effectively in English classrooms. Teaching English to language-minority students is, however, only part of what teachers should be striving to do. As educators, we must also work hard to ensure that the price these children pay for learning English is not the loss of their mother tongue and their cultural identity. We must also help all students to recognize the worth of all languages and to see fluency in another language as an advantage rather than a stigma.

RESOURCES

Books for Children

These books are about adjustment to American culture by immigrant children and language differences generally. Although some are guilty of providing "pat" answers to difficult and complex problems, they do raise important issues and can be used to discuss discrimination and help children learn respect for languages other than their own.

Atkinson, M. (1979). *Maria Teresa*. Chapel Hill, NC: Lollipop Power. [Gr. 1 -4]

Borlenghi, P. (1992). *From albatros to zoo: An alphabet book in five languages*. New York: Scholastic.

Bouchard, L. (1969). *The boy who wouldn't talk*. New York: Doubleday. [Gr. 4-7].

Castle, S. (1977). *Face talk, hand talk, body talk*. New York: Doubleday. [Gr. PreK-2]

Feelings, M. (1976). *Moja means one: Swahili counting book*. Garden City, NY: Dial. [Gr. K-3]

Gilson, J. (1985). *Hello, my name is Scrambled Eggs*. Fairfield, NJ: Lothrop. [Gr. 5-7]

Haskins, J. (1982). *The new Americans: Cuban boat people*. Hillside, NJ: Enslow. [Gr. 6-9]

Levine, E. (1989). *I hate English*. New York: Scholastic. [Gr. 1-3]

Lewiton, M. (1959). *Candita's choice*. New York: Harper & Row. [Gr. 4-6]

Lord, B. B. (1984). *In the year of the boar and Jackie Robinson*. New York: Harper & Row. [Gr. 4-6]

Michels, B., & White, B. (Eds.). (1983). *Apples on a stick: The folklore of black children*. East Rutherford, NJ: Coward-McCann. [Gr. 3-6]

Nye, N. S. (1994). *Sitti's secret*. New York: Four Winds Press. [Gr. K-3]

Paek, M. (1988). *Aekyung's dream*. San Francisco, CA: Children's Book Press. [Gr. 2-4]

Rosario, I. (1981). *Idalia's project ABC: An urban alphabet book in English and Spanish*. Orlando, FL: Holt, Rinehart and Winston.

Stanek, M. (1989). *I speak English for my mom*. Niles, IL: Whitman. [Gr. 1-3]

Surat, M. M. (1983). *Angel child, dragon child*. Milwaukee, WI: Raintree. [Gr. 3-5]

Wartski, M. C. (1980). *A long way from home*. Philadelphia, PA: Westminster. [Gr. 6-9]

Resources for Adults

In addition to the following, many of the citations in the reference section would also be helpful.

ALA/ALSC Committee on the Selection of Children's Books and Materials from Various Cultures. (1990). Distributors of children's foreign-language books: Update 1990. *Booklist, 86*, 2184-2185. This article categorizes children's foreign-language books by distributors and language. *Booklist* also regularly highlights current children's books that are written in a variety of languages.

Beilke, P., & Sciara, F. J. (1986). *Selecting materials for and about Hispanic and East Asian children and young people*. Hamden, CT: Library Professional Publications.

Center for New American Media. (Producer). Kolker, A., & Alvarez, L. (Directors). (1986). *American tongues*. [Film]. New York: Center for New American Media. An excellent film on American dialects and accents.

Heath, S. B. (1983). *Ways with words: Language, life and work in communities and classrooms*. Cambridge, England: Cambridge University Press. A study of children from two different social groups learning to use language. The politics and impact of language are explored.

Schon, I. (1991). Recent noteworthy books in Spanish for young children. *Young Children, 46*, 66.

References

Abramson, S., Seda, I., & Johnson, C. (1990). Literacy development in a multilingual kindergarten classroom. *Childhood Education, 67*(2), 68-72.

Adler, S. (1993). *Multicultural communication skills in the classroom*. Boston, MA: Allyn and Bacon.

Allen, D. (1996). Teaching with technology: Breaking the language barrier. *Teaching K-8, 26*(5), 16-18.

Cazden, C. B. (1988). *Classroom discourse*. Portsmouth, NH: Heinemann.

Cheng, L. L. (1987). *Assessing Asian language performance*. Rockville, MD: Royal Tunbridge Wells.

Collier, V. P. (1987). The effect of age on the acquisition of a second language for school. *New Focus: National Council for Bilingual Education, 2*, 1-5.

Daniels, H. A. (Ed.). (1990). *Not only English: Affirming America's multilingual heritage*. Urbana, IL: National Council of Teachers of English.

Farb, P. (1975). *Word play: What happens when people talk*. New York: Knopf.

Garcia, E. (1996). Preparing instructional professionals for linguistically and culturally diverse students. In J. Sikula (Ed.), *Handbook of research on teacher education* (2nd ed.) (pp. 802-813). New York: Macmillan.

Gardner, R. C., & Lambert, W. E. (1972). *Attitudes and motivation in second-language learning*. Rowley, MA: Newberry House.

Gersten, R. (1996). The double demands of teaching English language learners. *Educational Leadership, 53*, 18-22.

Grove, C. L. (1976). *Communications across culture*. Washington, DC: National Education Association.

Hall, E. T. (1973). *The silent language*. Garden City, NY: Anchor.

Hough, R. A., Nurss, J. R., & Enright, D. S. (1986). Story reading with limited English speaking children in the regular classroom. *The Reading Teacher, 39*(6), 510-514.

Hudelson, S. (1986). ESL children's writing: What we've learned, what we're learning. In P. Rigg & D. S. Enright (Eds.), *Children and ESL: Integrating perspectives* (pp. 23-54). Washington, DC: Teachers of English to Speakers of Other Languages.

Kottler, E. (1994). *Children with limited English: Teaching strategies for the regular classroom*. Thousand Oaks, CA: Corwin.

Moustafa, M. (1980). Picture books for oral language development for non-English speaking children: A bibliography. *The Reading Teacher, 33,* 914-919.

Myer, L. (1985). *Excellence in leadership and implementation: Programs for limited English proficient students.* San Francisco, CA: San Francisco Unified School District.

National Education Association. (1993). A bridge between cultures. *NEA Today: Special Edition, 12*(1), 38-39.

Newmark, E., & Asante, M. K. (1976). *Intercultural communication.* Urbana, IL: ERIC Clearinghouse on Reading and Communications Skills.

Perez, S. A. (1979). How to effectively teach Spanish-speaking children, even if you're not bilingual. *Language Arts, 56,* 159-162.

Ruiz, R. (1991). The empowerment of language-minority students. In C. E. Sleeter (Ed.), *Empowerment through multicultural education* (pp. 217-227). Albany, NY: State University of New York Press.

Soto, L. D. (1991). Understanding bilingual/bicultural young children. *Young Children, 46,* 30-36.

Taylor, O. L. (1986). A cultural and communicative approach to teaching standard English as a second dialect. In O. L. Taylor (Ed.), *Treatment of communication disorders in culturally and linguistically diverse populations* (pp. 153-178). San Diego, CA: College-Hill.

Tiedt, P. L., & Tiedt, I. M. (1990). *Multicultural teaching: A handbook of activities, information and resources.* Boston: Allyn & Bacon.

Valdez, G. (1990). Personal communication.

Waggoner, D., & O'Malley, J. M. (1985). Teachers of limited English proficient children in the United States. *NABE Journal, 9*(3), 25-42.

Welton, D. A. (1990, Fall). Language as a mirror of culture. *Educators' Forum,* p. 7.

Williams, S. W. (1991). Classroom use of African American language: Educational tool or social weapon. In C. E. Sleeter (Ed.), *Empowerment through multicultural education* (pp. 199-215). Albany, NY: State University of New York Press.

Willis, S. (1994). Teaching language-minority students. *Association for Supervision and Curriculum Development: Curriculum Update, 36*(5), 1-5.

Willis, S. (1996). Foreign languages: Learning to communicate in the real world. *Association for Supervision and Curriculum Development: Curriculum Update,* Winter.

Wong-Fillmore, L. (1985). When does teacher talk work as input? In S. Gass & C. Madden (Eds.), *Input in second language Acquisition* (pp. 17-50). Rowley, MA: Newbury.

Wong-Fillmore, L. (1989). Teaching English through content: Instructional reform in programs for language minority students. In J. Esling (Ed.), *Multicultural education and policy: ESL in the 1990s* (pp. 125-143). Toronto: OISE Press.

Wong-Fillmore, L. (1990). Now or later? Issues related to the early education of minority-group children. In C. Harris (Ed.), *Children at risk* (pp. 110-133). New York: Harcourt, Brace & Jovanovich.

Wong-Fillmore, L., & Valadez, C. (1986). Teaching bilingual learners. In M. Wittrock (Ed.), *Handbook on research in teaching* (pp. 648-684). New York: Macmillan.

Wyner, N. B. (1989, Summer). Educating linguistic minorities: Public education and the search for unity. *Educational Horizons,* 172-176.

Chapter 6

Gender Equity in the Classroom

Beverly Hardcastle Stanford

The audience of 3rd- through 6th-graders sit nearly shoulder to shoulder on the cafeteria floor and listen with remarkable politeness to their peers as they perform a medley on resistant musical instruments. The more prominent traits of race and ethnicity command an observer's attention before gender does. Nearly all the faces in the gathering are white, and almost half of the heads of hair are blond or light brown. The ethnic make-up is the photo negative of the groups in neighboring schools.

Later, in response to a request for a more culturally diverse setting for observing gender-fair teaching, a vivacious African American dean of education with ties to a wide network of talented African American teachers replies, "I know outstanding teachers who teach equitably, but their major concern is racism, not sexism." Her comments remind us that children may be victims of more than one bigotry—sexism, racism, classism, ethnic hostility.

We must recognize the unique and multilayered dimensions of prejudice. Only then can the significant problem of gender bias gain its needed focus.

The Problem

In the cafeteria, the children, sitting in crowded wavy rows that extend across the floor, have segregated themselves into linear groups—6 boys, 3 girls, 4 boys, 5 girls and so forth. The small orchestra is well-balanced in gender terms, but the 61-member choir has only 6 boys, who stand together on the right side of the group. Other than the clustering, the boys' behavior reflects a satisfactory comfort level. Their singing matches the girls' in effort and enthusiasm; their song gestures and signing of lyrics are in synchrony with the group. Apparently they are neither the choir's clowns nor its brow-beaten participants, but, no question, their limited number cannot go unnoticed.

Recent public and professional attention to gender bias has prompted a much needed strand of research on gender equity in schools. Much of this research focuses on gender-specific teacher-student interactions and differences in male and female academic achievements.

Research on Gender Equity

Teacher-student interactions. The two major patterns that emerged consistently in research studies on teacher-student interactions and gender discrimination during the mid-1980s and early '90s were: 1) teachers give boys more attention, both positive and negative, and 2) boys demand more teacher attention.

In a two-year study of teacher communication patterns with children in nine 1st- and nine 5th-grade classrooms, Phyllis Blumenfeld and her colleagues found that boys received a significantly greater portion of teacher communication and attention than girls. In the second year of the study, when the children were in the 2nd and 6th grade, the researchers found the same pattern and additionally noted that boys received more negative feedback on their conduct (Eccles & Blumenfeld, 1985).

Summarizing findings from the above study and those she conducted with other colleagues, Jacquelynne Eccles concluded that "1) males are yelled at and criticized publicly more than females and 2) males are more likely than females to monopolize teacher-student interaction time" (1989, p. 49). In her discussion of the extensive research on gender and classroom interactions, she offered a vivid illustration of inequity in class participation, describing a group of participants we can refer to as classroom "stars":

We have now observed in over 150 math classrooms in southeastern Michigan; in 40 of them, we coded every interaction the teacher had with each student over a ten-day period. Over half the students *never* talked to the teacher during the 10 days. Others had 14 or more interactions with the teacher *every hour*. Most of these latter students were male. (Eccles, 1989, p. 49)

In their early work in the field of gender equity, from 1980-1984, Myra and David Sadker studied classroom interactions in over 100 4th-, 6th- and 8th-grade classrooms in four states and the District of Columbia. In all subjects and at all three grade levels, they found that:

Male students were involved in more interactions than female students. It did not matter whether the teacher was Black or White, female or male; the pattern remained the same. Male students received more attention from teachers. (Sadker & Sadker, 1986, p. 512)

They found that boys called out and demanded their teachers' attention eight times more often than girls. Perhaps of more significance, when teachers responded to the called out answers they tended to accept boys' answers while correcting girls' behavior, advising them to raise their hands. The Sadkers concluded that "boys are being trained to be assertive; girls are being trained to be passive—spectators relegated to the sidelines of classroom discussion" (1986, p. 513).

They also found that boys received more specific, and consequently more instructive, feedback. They classified feedback into four groups: nonspecific acceptance (over half the comments), specific praise (approximately 10 percent), specific criticism (approximately 15 percent) and remediation with instructions designed to guide students to the correct response (over one-third). While less instructive, nonspecific acceptance comments were distributed fairly equitably; teachers gave boys significantly more praise, criticism and remediation.

Achievement in math and science. The fields of math and science were predominantly male domains in the mid-1980s and early 1990s. Less than 6 percent of the doctorates and less than 10 percent of the masters in engineering went to women in 1984 (Eccles, 1989, p. 36). Girls sought college entry with about one year less physical science and one-half year less of math than did boys (*Women and Minorities in Science and Engineering*, 1986). Girls' interest in science dropped by the end of 3rd grade, according to data collected by the National Assessment of Educational Progress, and by the end of the middle grades, most girls decide that science is not for them (*Harvard Education Letter*, May/June 1990). The area of computers also appeared to be an addition to the male domain. Only 24 percent of the children attending summer computer camps were girls (Kreinberg, Alper & Joseph, 1985).

Surprisingly, math achievement in the elementary and junior high years is relatively similar for boys and girls. Differences usually occur at the elementary level and tend to favor girls (Campbell, 1986). By high school, however, gender differences increase and clearly favor boys. Researchers attribute the phenomenon to girls being socialized away from math by their parents and teachers.

PROGRESS

In her 3rd-grade classroom, Carolyn, a teacher known for her gender-fair teaching, addresses her class of gifted students: "Ladies and Gentlemen, it's time to go over your homework. For the picture you drew of two scientists working on a project, what did you name your scientists?" All but two girls raise their hands. Carolyn moves around the room, calling on students in an unpredictable pattern.

Their answers:
   "Ben and Joe."
   "Bud and Bud."
   "John and Bob."
   "Brian and Kenny." (from Brian)
   "Whew. I have my work cut out for me," Carolyn says to herself and the observer.
   "Bob and Jenny."
   "Pammy and Jim."
   "Elliott and Elaine." (from Elliott)
   "Eric and Erin."
   "Courtney and Christina."
   "Michael and David."
   "Joseph and James."
   "Sally and Princess."
   "Pop and Corn."
   "Adam and I."
   Then Carolyn asks, "What did you notice about the scientists' names?" The children's answers come more slowly:
   Laura: "They sound scientific."
   Matthew: "Some were names in our class."
   Finally Carolyn observes, "I noticed that most of you named male or boy names rather than girl names. Even if you were a girl, you named boy names. There were only two exceptions; only two girls named two girls as scientists. Do you have an explanation for that?"
   A girl defends her selection, "I put a boy and a girl."
   "That's true," Carolyn agrees. "Some of you picked a boy and a girl." She continues, "But only two picked two girls. Do you have an explanation? Is there a reason why? What do you think?" More answers:
   Laura: "Maybe it's because there are more boy scientists than girl."
   Joseph: "There are more smarter boys than there are girls."
   Austin: "People think of boys being scientists more than girls."
   Carolyn: "Why do you imagine that's true?"
   Austin: "People generally think of boys as scientists."
   Carolyn: "What other kinds of things do people think of boys as generally being?"
   Kenny: "People working on cars."
   Kristin: "Firemen."
   Rikki: "Doctors and principals."
   Carolyn: "Now you have a doctor mom and a doctor dad, right? And you think of doctors more as men, is that right?"
   Rochelle: "Baseball players and race car drivers."
   Everyone has a chance to add to the discussion.

As the children's answers indicate, much work remains in the area of gender fairness. The gender-equity messages are clearer now, however, and efforts to communicate them to a broader audience are gaining momentum.

Grounding in Title IX

Title IX of the Education Amendments of 1972 (1976) is the major source for teachers to draw upon to determine their legal obligations regarding sexism and gender-role stereotyping in the classroom. The law states that, "No person shall on the basis of sex, be excluded from participation in, be denied the benefits of, or be subjected to discrimination under any education program or activity receiving federal financial assistance. . . . " (Title IX of the Education Amendments of 1972, 1976). Violations of the law can result in withholding of federal funds.

Reason for being. Title IX was drafted at a time when boys and girls received distinctively different education programs and opportunities. Financing and scheduling of athletic programs were dominated by male interests and participation, and most female athletes were unable to go far with their talents. In 1969, for example, the Syracuse, New York, school board allocated $90,000 for boys' extracurricular sports and $200 for girls' sports (Lever, 1978). In most schools, career counselors guided boys into professional fields and girls toward secretarial work, homemaking, nursing and teaching. Girls could not take industrial arts, boys could not take home economics classes and physical education classes were taught separately. Gender-role stereotyping was promoted both consciously and unconsciously to the detriment of girls especially, whose education and career options were consequently limited dramatically.

Extent of the law. The regulation applies to any educational institution, private or public, that receives financial aid from the federal government. "Educational institutions controlled by a religious organization holding religious tenets (such as the belief that sex segregation is divinely ordained) inconsistent with Title IX" (Williams, 1980, p. 152) are the only institutions excluded. The 1984 Supreme Court decision in *Grove City College v. Bell* determined that only the programs and activities receiving federal funding, and not the entire institutions, were subject to the terms of Title IX. The resulting reduction of the power of Title IX was significant.

Applying the law. The provisions of the law fall into three broad areas: admission of students, treatment of students and employment. The middle section provides answers to a variety of questions of interest and relevance to teachers and administrators. For instance, would educators be violating the law if:

- *For the same offense, they punished boys by having them stay after school and girls by having them remain in the classroom for recess?*
- *They established an all-male safety patrol?*
- *They had separate physical education classes?*
- *They used gender-biased tests?*
- *They kept a female student from playing on the football team?*
- *They used gender-biased texts?*

The answer to all but the last two of these questions is *yes*, they would be violating the terms of Title IX. Title IX specifically *prohibits*:

Provision of DIFFERENT aid, benefits, or services on the basis of sex, DENIAL of such aid, benefits, or services to persons of either sex, SEPARATE or DIFFERENT rules of behavior, punishments or other treatment, on the basis of sex, [and] LIMITATION of any right, privilege, advantage, or opportunity on the basis of sex. (Sadker & Sadker, 1982, p. 44)

While physical education classes need to be coeducational, segregation of the sexes can occur for team sports when selections are based on competitive skills. The law permits sepa-ration of the sexes for contact sports, but does not require it. Court cases challenging the contact sports provision resulted in the acceptance of qualified female players onto football teams because their schools did not have comparable teams for girls (Williams, 1980, pp. 154-155).

Title IX also requires counselors to give unbiased career and education guidance. In addition, the law prohibits schools from using gender-biased achievement, aptitude and interest tests.

Because of concern for interfering with the terms of the First Amendment, however, lawmakers did not forbid the use of textbooks and curriculum materials that contain gender bias and stereotyping. The Sadkers note the assumption in Title IX that "local education agencies will deal with the problem of sex bias in curriculum materials in the exercise of their general authority and control over course content" (1982, p. 45).

Landmark legislation. The spirit of Title IX and educators' and organizations' efforts to publicize evidence of gender inequities in schools affected the 1994 revision of the Elementary and Secondary Education Act (ESEA). The gender-equity amendments to the document resulted in the following provisions to require:

training to help teachers eliminate classroom practices that diminish girls' academic abilities and confidence; recruiting of female math and science teachers who can be role models to encourage girls' pursuit of math and science studies; training and technical assistance to combat sexual harassment; revitalizing the Women's Education Equity Act (WEEA) to research and disseminate model programs that address bias against girls and women in education; and assisting pregnant and parenting teens in dropout prevention programs to stay in school. (*PR Newswire*, October 5, 1994, p. 1)

Teachers should know about federally funded programs in their schools and be aware that they may include, among other gender-equity elements, resources to bring in trainers to teach them about gender-fair teaching strategies and sexual-harassment prevention.

Spreading the Word

A major leader in publicizing the problem of gender inequities in schools, and a significant contributor to the progress that has been achieved thus far, is the American Association of University Women. In the late 1980s, AAUW began an impressive research and action agenda on gender equity. AAUW publishes findings and recommendations from these efforts in reports, issue briefs, action guides, books and videotapes.

The most influential of these reports are *Shortchanging Girls, Shortchanging America* (1991); *How Schools Shortchange Girls: The AAUW Report* (1992b); *Hostile Hallways: The AAUW Survey on Sexual Harassment in America's Schools* (1993); and *Growing Smart: What's Working for Girls in School* (1995). The first report provided results of a national survey of 3,000 girls and boys ages 9-15 that sought information on students' schooling experiences, interests in math and science, and attitudes toward themselves, friends, family and careers. For the second report, Susan McGee Bailey and a team of researchers and writers reviewed over 1,300 articles, including hundreds of research studies, to evaluate the K-12 experiences of girls and boys. AAUW continued its exploration of students' school experiences by investigating the area of sexual harassment. Louis Harris and Associates, commissioned to conduct the national survey, surveyed 1,632 students in grades 8 through 11 in 79 public schools across the country. The fourth report marks the beginning of AAUW's efforts to determine and evaluate solutions. University of Minnesota researchers Sunny Hansen, Joyce Walker and Barbara Flom prepared a scholarly review of literature that examined factors promoting girls' healthy achievement and growth from kindergarten through 12th grade.

Focusing Concerns

Evaluating the progress in gender equity in the mid-1990s, Alice Ann Leidel, the President of the American Association of University Women's Educational Foundation observed:

We've seen the gender gap shrink in mathematics, with girls now achieving near the level of boys. We're seen at least a few female figures inserted alongside male figures in the history texts from which our children learn. And we've seen girls given new access to teacher attention and traditional male preserves like technology. . . . But gender equity is still a long way from being realized. . . . (AAUW, 1995, p. iv)

While research in recent years has broken little new ground, the confluences of results from earlier studies bring focus and credibility to a number of previously cited findings. Four areas of gender-equity research that merit special attention are girls' self-esteem in early adolescence, sexual harassment, boys' and girls' learning styles, and single-sex schools and classes.

Girls' drop in self-esteem. The finding that has provoked the most discussion and continued research relates to American girls' apparent drop in self-esteem as they enter adolescence. In a number of distinctive studies, researchers report evidence of girls' loss of voice and confidence in early adolescence.

In the American Association of University Women's 1990 national survey, both boys and girls agreed with the statement "I am happy the way I am" less frequently as they grew older. The drop for girls, however, is quite dramatic:

69 percent of elementary school boys and 60 percent of elementary school girls reported that they were 'happy the way I am;' among high school students the percentages were 46 percent for boys and only 29 percent for girls. (1992b, AAUW, p. 19)

In a 1986-1990 study of nearly 100 girls ages 7 through 18 conducted at Cleveland's Laurel School for girls, Lyn Mikel Brown, Carol Gilligan (1992) and their team of researchers and writers explored girls' transitions into adolescence. They discovered evidence of confusion about identity and experience and sometimes defensiveness.

In her 1987-91 study of girls' psychological development, Annie G. Rogers (1993) found girls ages 8 to 12 to be clearly confident and comfortable in speaking their minds, disagreeing with others and expressing their wishes and anger. In early adolescence, however, such assurance diminished and girls began punctuating their interview responses with phrases such as "I don't know" and "this probably doesn't make sense" (p. 272). Referring to the findings of her Harvard colleagues Brown and Gilligan, Rogers suggests that "girls lose not only clarity, self-confidence, and voice—but also their courage—as they come of age" (p. 272). Drawing on an early English definition of courage, "to speak one's mind by telling all one's heart," Rogers observes that "the ordinary courage of eight- to twelve-year-old girls becomes readily visible and audible." She expresses regret that over the centuries the definition of courage shifted to signify "the bravery and heroic valor of men" (p. 288), for with the change, the perception of young girls as courageous was lost to both men and women.

Sexual harassment. The AAUW study of sexual harassment in schools broke new ground. In 1993, Harris and Associates conducted a national survey of public school students in grades 8 through 11. The resulting report, *Hostile Hallways*, announced that four out of five students experienced some form of sexual harassment. Such sexual-harassment experiences ranged from receiving unwanted "sexual comments, jokes, gestures, or looks," to being "forced to do something sexual, other than kissing" (AAUW, 1993, p. 5). Two-thirds of the students reported experiencing the former, and 11 percent were victims of the latter. Surprisingly, 76 percent of boys and 85 percent of girls reported experiencing some form of sexual harassment. The first experience tended to occur in 6th through 9th grade, but a few students (6 percent) reported incidents of sexual harassment before 3rd grade. Only 7 percent told their teachers and 23 percent told their parents or other family member. The report stresses the need for a reduction in sexual harassment in schools for the benefit of both sexes.

Boys' and girls' learning styles. Some researchers in the 1990s offer conclusions regarding differences in boys' and girls' learning styles and others argue that learning styles are individual and idiosyncratic, rather than gender specific.

At a 1991 Educational Testing Service conference, Nancy Goldberger, an analyst for the Fielding Institute for Psychology and Human Development, reported:

Schools are geared more to the learning styles of white males, which tend to be individualistic and competitive. In contrast, many girls prefer cooperation over competition, acknowledging and building on others' ideas to define common meanings over individual contributions, and understanding over assessment. (*CQ Researcher*, 1994, p. 5)

Goldberger's observations fit well with those presented by Lever in her study of children's play. Lever hypothesized that one reason boys' recess games lasted longer than girls' was that when rules were broken boys continued to play while simultaneously engaging in a second game, a debate over the rules. In contrast, girls stopped their games to end a conflict. Goldberger proposes a related view regarding the differences in the ways boys and girls learn:

Girls tend to see the role of peers as support. Girls acknowledge the uncertainty of knowledge [and] put less emphasis on reconciling disagreement than on understanding where others are coming from. Boys tend to see the role of peers as challengers and partners in argument. One speaks to show what one knows; one argues with others to sharpen one's position. Devil's advocacy is a strategy that is far more comfortable for and utilized by boys and men than girls and women. (*CQ Researcher*, 1994, p. 5)

Girls in adolescence tend to attribute failures in math to a lack in ability, while boys blame the subject itself. Furthermore, "males are more apt than females to attribute their successes to ability" according to the authors of AAUW's report *How Schools Shortchange Girls* (1995, pp. 47-48). In science, adolescent boys are "more likely to guess and estimate answers [and] girls are more likely to work out the exact solution to problems," Carol Shakeshaft observes in *Theory into Practice*. She recommends that to improve test scores girls need to learn "to take risks, estimate answers, and take shortcuts in their problem solving" (1995, p. 75).

Shakeshaft warns, however, that "all kids need a range of skills. Boys need to work cooperatively; girls need to learn to compete" (cited in Tovey, 1995, p. 6). Similarly, after investigating students' perspectives on their learning, Nona Lyons encourages teachers and researchers to focus more on individualizing teaching and learning rather than on responding to proposed gender-based learning style differences (Tovey, 1995, p. 5).

Single-sex schools. Recent efforts to promote gender equity through single-sex schools and single-sex classes and groupings within coeducational schools have been both hailed and criticized. Experiments in single-sex schools and classrooms for African American boys have been launched in Detroit, Baltimore, Milwaukee and Dade County (Florida), attracting national attention, prompting heated debates and provoking litigation. Supporters see the benefits of focusing on a group that has consistently failed in the school system (that the school system has failed) and emphasize the need for male models and male-only environments for boys raised in "female-dominated, poverty stricken homes" (Greathouse & Sparling, 1993). Observers, supportive of providing educational assistance for low-income children, are outraged that the African American male-only academies overlook the needs of African American girls in the same neighborhoods. They echo the past by questioning whether separate could be equal and claim that the civil rights of girls are violated, while the boys are stigmatized as needing special treatment.

Research on single-sex education also has focused on students in women's colleges. A review of literature on gender equity conducted by Susan Klein and Patricia Ortman (1994, p. 17) with 12 other recognized researchers outlines compelling findings regarding female students in women's colleges—enhanced self-esteem, increased assertiveness and greater class participation. These advantages presumably exist for girls in elementary and secondary schools, as well (Sadker & Sadker, 1994).

AAUW takes a cautious stand on single-sex classes, seeing merit in them for short-term solutions either "to redress past inequities in areas like math and science" or "to prepare girls to participate fully in mixed-gender classrooms" (AAUW, 1995, p. 10). In the AAUW report *Growing Smart, What's Working for Girls in School*, the authors advise educators to seek legal counsel to determine if their single-sex classes are in compliance with Title IX. If the classes are specifically created to respond to sex differences in achievement and if course enrollment is open to male and female students and teachers, violations of Title IX are less likely.

Critics of single-sex classes include Bailey, the principal author of *How Schools Short-change Girls*, who argues that "single-sex classes can send a message that girls need special attention, which can be undermining rather than empowering" (Tovey, 1995, p. 4). Valerie Lee, a researcher outspokenly against single-sex classrooms, complains, "The problem is that there is a basic assumption at work here—that males will dominate—and that that is okay" (Tovey, 1995, p. 4). She argues that male dominance should be challenged, not accommodated by placing its victims in separate environments.

PROMISE

Carolyn shifts the discussion focus from "What other kinds of things do people think of boys as generally being?" to "Is there anything that we named that girls can't be?"

"Football players," a boy calls out.

"Do you remember how Renee was spiraling that football out, and she was doing good. You know what, Renee, if you wanted to . . . just something to kind of think about."

Autumn: "Professional football players."

Kristin: "Girls can't be in the army."

Several children protest loudly. Carolyn reminds the class that their visitor the previous day was a woman teacher who had been in the army, and she named another woman teacher in the school who had military experience.

Carolyn shifts the discussion once more. "Who in here might consider being a scientist? Please stand if your hand is up. [Nearly all of the boys and several girls stand.] Now point to someone seated who might be a good scientist. If someone pointed to you, stand up and everyone else please sit down. Ah, Kristin is standing. What is it about Kristin that makes you think she would be a good scientist?"

"Well, she's really smart."

"She could help a lot of people make friends."

"Is that important to be a scientist?" Carolyn asks the children.

"Yes. They need friends to help them."

Carolyn continues the discussion, showing children new reflections of themselves and exploring possibilities for their futures.

Later, at recess, Carolyn coaches girls to be assertive. Admiring the coeducational make-up of a vigorous game of four square, Carolyn explains that earlier in the year boys dominated the game. The girls had told Carolyn that they wanted to play, but the boys threw "hardees." Carolyn noted that the L. A. Rams don't ask their opponents not to hit hard, and advised the girls to learn to throw "hardees" if they wanted to play four square. The girls took her advice and now were playing with the same exuberance and aggression as the boys.

Principles To Guide Practice

Drawing on over 500 1989-94 academic studies and youth-development project reports, the authors of the AAUW publication *Growing Smart: What's Working for Girls in School* identified five central themes that contribute to "the achievement and healthy development of girls from kindergarten through grade 12" (1995, p. vi). The five themes, which the authors note can be equally effective for boys, are:

- Celebrate girls' strong identity
- Respect girls as central players
- Connect girls to caring adults
- Ensure girls' participation and success
- Empower girls to realize their dreams. (1995, p. 1)

The report advises teachers to set high expectations for girls and to be careful not to give too much help. It encourages teachers to conduct research on multiculturalism and gender in their own classrooms, and invites them to share what they learn with AAUW. A directory of over two dozen model programs that implement gender-equity principles is included.

PRACTICE

How can practice benefit from the gender-equity research findings and follow the gender-fair guidelines suggested in professional reports? Specific practices and an illustrative case study of gender-fair teaching are presented here.

Classroom Procedures and Teaching Strategies

Equalizing teacher-student interactions. A number of strategies can be used to counteract the tendency for males to dominate classroom interactions. First, teachers need to become conscious of the degree and type of attention they give to members of each gender in classroom interactions. The Sadkers found that once aware of their unconscious inequitable treatment of students, teachers were able to enact change remarkably quickly. They also found that the best way of increasing teachers' awareness in this area was to tally the number of times the teacher called on a boy or a girl and note whether the teacher's response was acceptance, praise, remediation or criticism.

Resisting the dominance of several "star" students, usually male, in teacher-student interactions is a challenge. Ignoring stars when they call out is one approach. Calling on students according to a systematic and equitable plan is another. Teachers may use a pattern of calling on students alphabetically, following the chronology of birthdays or asking students to call on a classmate of the other gender for the next response.

Some teachers make the process even more deliberate. When they call on students in a recitation exercise or a discussion, they draw from a deck of index cards containing the names of students in the class, making certain to reinsert each used card into the deck so that participants will not lose interest and alertness. Others give each student in class several "participation chips," which they are required to use before the end of a discussion. This procedure limits the number of contributions star students can make and forces reluctant students to participate. Of course, the quality of the discussion and individual needs must also be considered when using this approach. Children that contribute to the interest level and liveliness of a discussion can choose several additional chips and shy students can opt for only one chip. Even minor adjustments like these can set off a process of change. Researchers report that if girls see other girls contribute to a discussion, they are more likely to participate themselves (*CQ Researcher*, 1994, p. 7).

Varying teaching strategies. Using strategies such as cooperative learning, team learning, and leaderless student discussions takes teachers out of the role of attention dispenser and requires more students to participate actively. To prevent students from replicating the tendency toward male dominance in these strategies, the functional roles should be changed frequently. In a cooperative learning group, for example, on one day a boy may be the leader, a girl the recorder, a boy the peacemaker and a girl the supply monitor, with the roles rotating on the following day.

Leaderless student discussions, also referred to as fishbowl discussions, can promote equity and be surprisingly effective with older students. In this approach, a small group of students prepare to discuss a common reading that the other students have not seen. Their efforts include either a written response to the reading or answers to a set of analytical and evaluative questions related to the reading. The prepared students form a small discussion circle, and the teacher and the remainder of the class form a circle surrounding them. One inner-circle student gives an overall summary of the reading for the benefit of the students in the outer circle. Then, the inner-circle students discuss the points that they addressed in their papers, while the outer-circle students listen and note any questions they have. When the discussion reaches a lull, outer-circle students ask questions to clarify their vicarious understanding of the reading. Teachers should move out of the line of vision of students who may address them rather than their peers in the inner circle. When students realize that they are the ones expected to talk, their participation increases. Teachers are free to keep a tally of participation and, at the end of the discussion, may ask non-participants for their opinions, thus advancing equity.

Countering Self-Imposed Sexism

Early-childhood sexism. When kindergarten and early childhood teachers see children in their care behaving in gender stereotypical ways, they need not blame themselves or become discouraged. The children are responding naturally to a major developmental need, that of establishing their gender identity. What should concern teachers and other adults are the parameters our culture has placed on the roles of males and females. Do the gender roles to which children in this age group rigorously seek to conform limit, stress or stretch them? What answers do we give when children ask, "Can a boy do that?" and "Is it all right for a girl to do that?" Selma Greenberg warns:

If we accept the verdict of both lay and professional persons that the early childhood years are not only important in themselves but that their effects have lifelong impact, we must view seriously what children do during these years and perhaps view even more seriously what they do not do or avoid doing. (1985, p. 458)

Guidelines and specific activities to help young children see more equitable gender roles are given in the book *Anti-bias Curriculum: Tools for Empowering Young Children* (Derman-Sparks & the ABC Task Force, 1989), in which the authors encourage teachers to expand children's play options and their awareness of gender roles. They suggest that teachers rearrange the play areas and supplement the costumes and materials they have in them. For instance, for the dramatic play center teachers can:

Put the woodworking table and tools into the "house" for making home repairs as well as wood constructions; put a typewriter, adding machine, and other materials in a "study". . . . Put the block area next to the dramatic play area for building work places (a market, a hospital, a gas station with mechanics). (Derman-Sparks & the ABC Task Force, 1989, p. 51)

While recognizing and wanting to preserve the value of free play for children, the authors suggest that at times teachers can intervene and guide children to activities that develop new skills. To expand children's awareness of gender roles, the authors urge teachers to use literature that breaks down stereotypes (see resource list at end of chapter).

Strengthening girls' transitions into early adolescence. According to Gilligan (1990), women teachers of 11- and 12-year-old girls have unique opportunities to assist girls with their transition into adolescence. Such teachers should first reflect on themselves, examining the model of adult women that they convey to their students, and then openly value the thinking of girls. They should encourage girls to express their ideas and risk disagreeing with others. Male teachers can help by encouraging their female students in similar ways and by being attuned to girls' psychological dilemma—the conflict they encounter between expressing themselves authentically and assertively as they had as girls or silencing themselves in order to be accepted as young women. Men and women can expand their awareness of girls' problems during adolescence by reading such books as the popular *School Girls: Young Women, Self-Esteem, and the Confidence Gap* (Orenstein, 1994).

Teaching about sexism directly. In *Failing at Fairness*, the Sadkers suggest asking students "to list twenty famous women from American history [who are] not in sports or entertainment [or] presidents' wives unless they are clearly famous in their own right" (1994, p. 7). The exercise is remarkably effective in demonstrating the invisibility of women in textbooks and curricula, and it can motivate students to correct the imbalance by doing independent research. Teachers may also invite to their classrooms individuals in nontraditional careers who can describe not only their careers, but also any discrimination experiences encountered in their studies and work. Such visits can be the springboard for class discussions about how we can all work for change.

Students can learn about gender inequity directly by doing field work, such as interviewing people in the community who work in nontraditional jobs and evaluating their textbooks or magazine articles to determine bias. They can conduct mini-research projects on gender inequity by observing in classrooms, lunchrooms and on playgrounds to see whether discrimination is occurring.

Creating Gender-Fair Classrooms

In addition to the strategies and procedures recommended above, certain elements in the classroom environment will contribute to the level of equity in classrooms. These include the teacher, the physical environment and the curricular materials.

The teacher. Teachers who actively commit to creating gender-fair environments can make a difference. Knowledge of the existence of sexism, sensitivity to evidence of it and a desire to counteract it are prerequisites for any effort to make a classroom climate gender fair.

In some areas, teachers need to provide more than equal treatment. Since "equity means freedom for both sexes to choose school and career activities without social censure" (Linn & Petersen, 1985, p. 53) and some school subjects and careers have been stereotyped as being either masculine or feminine, teachers must actively encourage students to use their abilities and talents. Of particular concern are girls' low confidence, motivation and performance in areas of math and science. Teachers must attempt to promote girls' appreciation of math and science, help them find the relevance of those subjects in their daily lives and encourage them to consider themselves as potential mathematicians and scientists. Fortunately, because of the seriousness of the problem, teachers now have access to organizations, companies, projects and resources devoted to helping parents and educators provide girls with equitable learning opportunities in math, science and, more recently, computers and educational technology (see resource list at end of chapter).

Finally, teachers must pay attention to their attitudes, the language they use and the models they present to students. Their own biases and prejudices will be conveyed nonverbally or by an inadvertent phrase or a limiting word of counsel. The specific language teachers use is subtly powerful in defining the world to children and showing them their place in it. Taking time to adjust habitual language and learn new terms may seem wasteful and superficial to teachers, but once they get past the first awkwardness of using *mail carrier* for *mailman*, *police officer* for *policeman*, *spokesperson* for *spokesman*, *humanity* for *mankind* and *nurturing* for *mothering*, they may notice that their own thinking changes. More important, they will acquire the habit of scrutinizing their speech for gender-discriminating or stereotyping expressions, and, consequently, will find it easier to detect and correct the language of others that limits, ignores or stereotypes either gender. How teachers respond when they encounter speech or behaviors that are gender discriminating or stereotyping will teach students more than any planned lessons on equity.

Equitable environment. The physical environment of a classroom reflects the equitability of its climate. Desks arranged in groupings, mixing boys and girls, indicate that both groups have value and should speak to each other and work together. Bulletin boards and display tables that advertise the ideas and accomplishments of men and women in all areas of the curriculum present a balanced picture of education for boys and girls. Events from the world beyond the classroom relayed in newspaper and magazine clippings can remind both girls and boys of the seriousness of their classroom learning.

Teachers must take care that the imprint they place on the environment is broad and inclusive. Male teachers whose visual displays neglect literature and art and female teachers who similarly underplay science and math perpetuate stereotypes that equitable classroom teachers seek to destroy. Androgyny, the incorporation of positive masculine *and* feminine characteristics, can be the guide word as teachers select subjects and materials to highlight in their classrooms.

Here, too, teachers need to be on guard for stereotyped gender images. Pictures of women in the roles of homemaker, nurse, teacher and secretary and men in the roles of doctor, minister and construction worker should be used sparingly. Less obvious stereotypes to avoid are the pictures of women with children, men with adults, women in passive postures, men in the midst of activity and men as the only ones in leadership roles.

Curricular materials. Nondiscriminatory curricular materials can also contribute to a sense of equity in classrooms. In their earlier book, *Sex Equity Handbook for Schools* (1982), the Sadkers provide specific guidelines for evaluating books, textbooks and instructional materials to detect biases and stereotyping. The broad areas they highlight are invisibility, the underrepresentation of women and minorities; stereotyping, portraying women and men in rigid roles; imbalance/selectivity, presenting only one side of an issue; unreality, interpreting history and contemporary life without reference to discrimination and prejudice; fragmentation/isolation, treating issues related to minorities and women as tacked-on sections separate from main content; and linguistic bias, using masculine terms and pronouns such as *forefathers*, *mankind* and the generic *he* (1982, pp. 72-73). Where these occur, teachers may address the sexism directly and conduct lessons or discussions on subtle forms of discrimination and their consequences. Teachers can also supplement biased instructional materials with books, magazine features and news articles that counter discriminatory information and images.

Illustrative Views of Gender-Fair Teaching

Carolyn DeMoss's teaching strategies and classroom environment provide gender-fair models to consider.

A 2nd grade in June. The temporary classroom that houses Carolyn's 2nd-grade class seems to spill over with projects from the year's activities. The busy walls and side tables are testimony to the children's productivity.

"Absolutely Amazing" is the headline for one bulletin board displaying submarine stories written by boys and girls in the class. The blackboard, the length of the room and focal point of the classroom, is nearly filled with assignments and reminders. In one corner is the announcement that Eli is "Queen for the Day" and Travis is "King for the Day." To the right of the blackboard is a news bulletin board with clippings about Mars, hostages and pollution; a separate section features a newspaper article about a potter who had visited their classroom.

A small bookcase and a greeting card display case, both filled with paperback books, convert one corner into a library. A number of the books in the collection reflect Carolyn's desire to promote gender equity. They twist tales in a new way: Sleeping Ugly, Sam Johnson and the Blue Ribbon

Quilt, The Dallas Titans Get Ready for Bed, The Paper Bag Princess, Brave Irene *and* My Mom Travels a Lot.

Two other books require only skim readings to find messages that could be used to elicit exciting class discussions on stereotypes and equity. Tiger Flower *describes a land where "everything is turned around, where nothing is the way it should be or the way it once was." Large things become small and small things become large, so the tiger becomes a gentle, flower-loving king of the grass, and butterflies sail boats with their wings.*

Piggybook *is the story of a mother and wife who tires of doing all the housework in addition to her work outside the home. She disappears one day, leaving her spoiled sons and husband a note telling them that they are pigs. They fend for themselves poorly, eventually taking on the form and habits of pigs and nearly die. She reappears; they are grateful, beg her to stay, continue to do the housework, return to human form, let her fix the car and everyone is happy.*

Carolyn is using her break period to prepare for a science class. She places a dead bee on a sheet of paper on each child's desk. Before she finishes, her students return. Thirty-one 2nd-graders enter the classroom, singly or in small groups of boys, girls or both. Winded from their physical education class, they speak in breathy bursts, comfortable with each other and their teacher, and make their way to their places in the tight United Nations arrangement of desks, which alternates boy, girl, boy, girl. The children respond to the specimens on their desk tops with much animation.

Calming them, Carolyn calls out slowly, "Who is ready for a science class? Hold on to your bees." She then whirs a mechanical bee on a string about her head, its hum quieting the group, and walks around the room, finally stopping in front of one child's desk.

Emphasizing the word "scientist," she directs the child to, "Please pass every scientist in the room a piece of this cut-up honeycomb." She repeats this procedure three more times, asking two boys and two girls to assist in distributing the honeycomb pieces and small magnifying glasses.

As Carolyn conducts her science lesson, she calls on children in unpredictable ways, managing to distribute attention equally among the boys and girls. After asking a question, she looks across the room of waving arms to a child whose hands are folded on her desk, "Sasha, would you call on someone for the answer?" The raised hands and stretching bodies shift toward Sasha.

Carolyn encourages the children to cooperate with each other. "Go show him how you found that." When a boy can't answer her question, she tells him, "Go get someone to whisper in your ear and then tell us."

Toward the end of the lesson, she focuses their attention on the value of learning science and does some active, gender-equitable career education. "When you grow up, what kind of a career, occupation could you have for which you would need information like this?"

"A beekeeper."

"Yes. Could anyone be a beekeeper?"

"Yes!"

A 4th grade in September. *It is the fourth day of school; Carolyn seems to have made the adjustment to a higher grade level with ease. She leads a discussion of the book* Call It Courage, *guiding the students to examine not only the bold actions of the main character, but also his feelings of fear. She thus teaches, consciously or unconsciously, a nonstereotyping perspective on the main character, highlighting his humanness in being both brave and fearful. "Ladies and gentlemen, think of a time when you have been afraid, afraid for your own safety's sake." She then directs students to tell their experiences of being afraid to other students in their desk groups. Everyone takes a turn.*

Minutes later, recess shows a clear contrast in the students' interactions. They immediately segregate into gender groups. Most of the boys run to a distant field to play soccer and most of the girls lock arms for a game of their own or huddle around Carolyn, moving with her like appendages as she monitors the playground activities on her duty day. One small group is integrated, mixing two girls with three boys. It passes by in a blur as one of the girls clutching a football races from her pursuers.

Seeing Carolyn's encouragement of equity, it is easy to imagine the life lessons her students will gain in her classrooms. Less predictable is how or whether their recess interactions will change. The girl with the football hinted of hope and the more recent coeducational four square game in which girls had learned to throw "hardees" offers more promise still.

RESOURCES

Books for Children

Ackerman, K. (1992). *When momma retires.* New York: Alfred A. Knopf

Bauer, C. F. (1986). Ill. by N. W. Parker. *My mom travels a lot.* New York: Viking.

Browne, A. (1989). *Piggybook.* New York: Alfred A. Knopf.

Cooney, B. (1982). *Miss Rumphius.* New York: Viking Penguin.

Ernst, L. C. (1983). *Sam Johnson and the blue ribbon quilt.* New York: Lothrop, Lee & Shepard Books.

Fireside, B. J. (1994). *Is there a woman in the house—or senate?* Morton Grove, IL: A. Whitman & Co.

Fitzhugh, L. (1964). *Harriet the spy.* New York: Harper.

George, J. C. (1972). *Julie of the wolves.* New York: Harper.

Hoffman, M. (1991). Ill. by C. Binch. *Amazing Grace.* New York: Dial.

Jukes, L. (1995). Ill. by S. Keeter. *I'm a girl.* Boca Raton, FL: Cool Kids Press.

Kongsburg, E. L. (1967). *From the mixed-up files of Mrs. Basil E. Frankweiler.* New York: Atheneum.

Kuskin, K. (1986). Ill. by M. Simont. *The Dallas Titans get ready for bed.* New York: Harper & Row.

Lasker, J. (1979). *Mothers can do anything.* Chicago: Albert Whitman.

Little, J. (1991). Ill. by J. Wilson. *Jess was the brave one.* New York: Viking.

MacLachlan, P. (1985). *Sarah, plain and tall.* New York: Harper.

Martin, B., Jr., & Archambault, J. (1986). *White dynamite and Curly Kid.* New York: Henry Holt.

Merriam, E. (1989). *Mommies at work.* New York: Simon.

Munsch, R. N. (1980). Ill. by M. Martchenko. *The paper bag princess.* Toronto, Canada: Annick Press Ltd.

O'Dell, S. (1960). *Island of the blue dolphins.* Boston: Houghton Mifflin.

Rappaport, D. (1991). *Living dangerously: American women who risked their lives for adventure.* New York: Harper Collins.

Saabin, F. (1983). Ill. by K. Milone. *Amelia Earhart: Adventure in the sky.* Mahwah, NJ: Troll Associates.

Schoop, J. (1986). Ill. by L. Beingessner. *Boys don't knit.* Trenton, NJ: Africa World Press, Inc.

Stamm, C. (1990). Ill. by J. and M. Tseng. *Three strong women: A tall tale from Japan.* New York: Viking.

Steig, W. (1986). *Brave Irene.* Toronto, Canada: Collins Publishers.

Vavra, R. (1968). Ill. by F. Cowles. *Tiger flower.* New York: Reynal & Co.

Warburg, S. S. (1965). Ill. by J. Chwast. *I like you.* Boston: Houghton Mifflin.

Yolen, J. (1981). Ill. by D. Stanley. *Sleeping ugly.* New York: Coward McCann.

Resources for Educators

Campbell, P. B. & Storo, J. N. (1996). *Math and science for the coed classroom.* Newton, MA: (Set of four pamphlets available from WEEA Equity Resouce Center Education Development Center, 55 Chapel Street, Suite 200, Newton, MA 02158-1060).

Derman-Sparks, L., & the ABC Task Force. (1989). *Anti-bias curriculum: Tools for empowering young children.* Washington, DC: National Association for the Education of Young Children.

Erickson, T. (1986). *Off and running, the computer off-line activities book.* Berkeley, CA: Regents, University of California.

Grayson, D. A. & Martin, M. D. (1996). *Gender/ethnic expectations and student achievement (GESA): Teacher handbook.* (Available from GrayMill Publications, 31630 Railroad Canyon, Canyon Lake, CA, 92587.

Grossman, H., & Grossman, S. H. (1994). *Gender issues in education.* Boston: Allyn & Bacon.

Klein, S. S. (Ed.). (1985). *Handbook for achieving sex equity through education.* Baltimore, MD: John Hopkins University Press.

Sadker, M., & Sadker, D. (1982). *Sex equity handbook for schools* (2nd ed.) New York: Longman.

Solnick, J., Langbort, C., & Day, L. (1982). *How to encourage girls in math and science.* Englewood Cliffs, NJ: Prentice-Hall.

Women's Equity for Educators Publishing Center. (1995). *Gender equity for educators, parents, and community.* Newton, MA: Author.

Other Curricular Resources

Educational Equity Concepts. 114 East 32nd Street. New York, NY 10016

EQUALS. Lawrence Hall of Science, University of California, Berkeley, CA 94720.

FAMILY MATH. Lawrence Hall of Science, University of California, Berkeley, CA 94720.

National Women's History Project. 7738 Bell Road, Windsor, CA 95492-8518.

The Guide to Math & Science Reform. The Annenberg/CPB Math and Science Project, P.O. Box 2345, South Burlington, VT 05407.

Women's Educational Equity Act World Wide Web Site. http://www.edc.org/CEEC/WEEA.

References

American Association of University Women. (AAUW). (1991). *Shortchanging girls, shortchanging America: A nationwide poll to assess self-esteem, educational experiences, interest in math and science, and career aspirations of girls and boys ages 9-15*. Washington, DC: Author.

American Association of University Women (AAUW). (1992a). *Creating a gender-fair multicultural curriculum*. (AAUW Issue Brief). Washington, DC: The AAUW Educational Foundation.

American Association of University Women. (AAUW). (1992b). *How schools shortchange girls: The AAUW report*. (Researched by The Wellesley College Center for Research on Women). Washington, DC: The AAUW Educational Foundation.

American Association of University Women. (AAUW). (1993). *Hostile hallways: The AAUW survey on sexual harassment in America's schools*. (Researched by Harris/Scholastic Research). Washington, DC: The AAUW Educational Foundation.

American Association of University Women (AAUW). (1995). *Growing smart: What's working for girls in schools*. (Researched by Sunny Hansen, Joyce Walker, & Barbara Flom). Washington, DC: The AAUW Educational Foundation.

Brown, L. M., & Gilligan, C. (1992). *Meeting at the crossroads: Women's psychology and girls' development*. New York: Ballantine Books.

Campbell, P. (1986). What's a nice girl like you doing in a math class? *Phi Delta Kappan, 67* (7), 516-520.

CQ Researcher. (1994, June 3). Education and gender, CQ Researcher, 4(21), 1-22.

Derman-Sparks, L., & the ABC Task Force. (1989). *Anti-bias curriculum: Tools for empowering young children*. Washington, DC: National Association for the Education of Young Children.

Eccles, J. (1989). Bringing young women to math and science. In M. Crawford & M. Gentry (Eds.), *Gender and thought: Psychological perspectives* (pp. 36-58). New York: Springer-Verlag.

Eccles, J., & Blumenfeld, P. (1985). Classroom experiences and student gender: Are there differences and do they matter? In L. C. Wilkinson & C. B. Marrett (Eds.), *Gender influences in classroom interaction* (pp. 79-114). Orlando, FL: Academic Press.

Gilligan, C. (1990). *Making connections: The relational worlds of adolescent girls at Emma Willard School*. Cambridge, MA: Harvard University Press.

Greenberg, S. (1985). Educational equity in early education environments. In S. S. Klein (Ed.), *Handbook for achieving sex equity through education* (pp. 457-469). Baltimore, MD: Johns Hopkins University Press.

Greathouse, B., & Sparling, S. (1993). African American male-only schools: Is that the solution? *Childhood Education, 69*(3), 131-132.

Harvard Education Letter. (1990, May/June). 6(3), 1-8.

Klein, S. S., Ortman, P. E., with Campbell, P., Greenberg, S., Hollingsworth, S., Jacobs, J., Kachuck, B., McClelland, A., Pollard, D., Sadker, D., Sadker, M., Schmuck, P., Scott, E., Wiggins, J., et al. (1994). Continuing the journey toward gender equity. *Educational Researcher, 23*(8), 13-21.

Kreinberg, N., Alper, L., & Joseph, H. (1985, March). Computers and children: Where are the girls? *PTA Today*, 13-15.

Lever, J. (1978). Sex differences in the complexity of children's play and games. *American Sociological Review, 43*, 471-483.

Linn, M. C., & Petersen, A. C. (1985). Facts and assumptions about the nature of sex differences. In S. S. Klein (Ed.), *Handbook for achieving sex equity through education* (pp. 457-469). Baltimore, MD: Johns Hopkins University Press.

Orenstein, P. (1994). *School girls: Young women, self-esteem, and the confidence gap.* (In Association with AAUW). New York: Doubleday.

PR Newswire, October 5, 1994: http://www. NlightN. com. ESEA. [article] Congress passes historic gender equity provisions in education bill: AAUW applauds recognition of girls in education reform.

Rogers, A. G. (1993). Voice, play, and a practice of ordinary courage in girls' and women's lives. *Harvard Educational Review, 63*(3), 265-295.

Sadker, M., & Sadker, D. (1982). *Sex equity handbook for schools* (2nd ed.) New York: Longman.

Sadker, M., & Sadker, D. (1986). Sexism in the classroom: From grade school to graduate school. *Phi Delta Kappan, 67*(7), 512-515.

Sadker, M., & Sadker, D. (1994). *Failing at fairness: How our schools cheat girls.* New York: Touchstone.

Shakeshaft, C. (1995). Reforming science education to include girls. *Theory into Practice, 34*(1), 74-79.

Title IX of the Education Amendments of 1972. (1976). S901, 20 U.S.C. S1681(a).

Tovey, R. (1995). A narrowly gender-based model of learning may end up cheating all students. *Harvard Education Letter, 9*(4), 3-6.

Williams, P. (1980). Laws prohibiting sex discrimination in the schools. In J. Stockard, P. Schmuck, K. Kempner, P. Williams, S. Edson, & M. Smith (Eds.), *Sex equity in education* (pp. 143-164). New York: Academic Press.

Women and minorities in science and engineering. (1986, January). (NSF 86-301). Washington, DC: National Science Foundation.

Author's note

The author expresses appreciation to Carolyn DeMoss, the gifted elementary teacher who shared her classroom so generously and modeled equitable teaching so naturally. She also thanks her Azusa Pacific University colleagues: Professor Maria A. Pacino, for her alert interest in this pursuit, Dean Alice Watkins, for her perspective and encouragement, and Provost A. J. Anglin and Associate Provost Patricia Anderson for their kind support of this work.

Chapter 7

Integrating Anti-Bias Education

James J. Barta

We have all read of schools around the United States where metal detection devices at the entrances screen for guns or knives. This is a disturbing reflection of the violence and fear that are present in far too many of our communities. Most agree that actions like this must be taken to stem the overt violence taking place in schools causing physical injury or even the death of our children. Yet, is it not ironic that social weapons such as racism, sexism and classism, whose violence may not be as immediately overt in our communities but can be equally as damaging, are carried freely and often unchallenged by students, teachers, administrators, staff and parents?

While the multicultural emphasis in contemporary education is well intentioned, it too often fails to address prejudice and the discrimination people may practice when responding to group differences. Teachers select literature for their classrooms that describes a number of diverse populations. Stories about children of many racial/ethnic groups and of children with disabilities may be commonly used. Current textbooks show boys and girls of color involved in meaningful daily activities and free of stereotypic gender-related job roles. Is the presentation of these differences enough? People saying or doing things differently are not the real issue. If group variations were viewed as merely different ways that people do the same things, then inequity and prejudice would not exist. It is the biased responses to variations that pose problems. Judgments about diversity, not diversity itself, is the cause of the turmoil (Phillips, 1988).

The goal of the anti-bias educator is to help all children learn to respect differences and work to identify and reduce oppressive attitudes and behaviors (Derman-Sparks, 1991). Educators may be concerned that anti-bias instruction is just one more element to add to an already overloaded schedule. Anti-bias education can be made a part of the curriculum, however, by integrating it into other academic content that must be shared. Rather than minimizing other educational goals, the integration of anti-bias curriculum can enrich the content. Through anti-bias curriculum children learn to think more critically, empathize with others, get along with others who have different points of views and cultural traditions, and take pride in their own heritage.

LESSONS IN ANTI-BIAS EDUCATION

The authors of the preceding chapters have described ways teachers can help illuminate our common bonds, validate the experiences of all children and empower the learner to question and challenge prejudice and discrimination. The anti-bias integration lessons and activities for elementary and middle school children described in this chapter will help teachers explore the interrelations between subject areas and an anti-bias perspective (Pappas, Kiefer & Levstik, 1990).

Mathematics

All humans have the potential for developing ways (consistent with their culture and environment) to understand and apply their mathematical reasoning as they tackle the problems of daily living. In most elementary math curricula, however, mathematics is presented as an enterprise removed from everyday life. Moreover, the significant contributions of women and nonEuropeans are seldom discussed. [Mathematicians included in the textbooks are usually male and European (e.g., Pythagoras, Thales, Euclid) and this has the effect of distorting children's knowledge about how math has evolved and who contributed to this evolution (Barta 1995).]

Children need to understand that each group's mathematical contribution reflects a link between the need for and the use of the mathematical technique within the context of the culture that developed it (D'Ambrosio, 1987). Several "real world" examples can be used to make this point. Masingila (1992), for example, describes the mathematical inventiveness of carpet layers who develop their own techniques for accurately carpeting irregularly shaped areas of floors. Brazilian street children who struggle to earn a living selling gum and candy have also developed nonstandard, yet sophisticated and reliable, procedures for mentally computing change for their customers (Saxe, 1988).

Culturally relevant problems. Educators can help children understand the cultural context of mathematics by challenging them to develop mathematical problems that reflect their own experiences. Students may create culturally specific problems around games or sports, production and harvesting of local crops, handicrafts, cooking or shopping. Teachers can help children understand that all people use mathematics, but may use it in different ways and for different purposes.

For exceptional students who often learn their math in resource rooms removed from the regular classroom and curriculum, this problem-focused, culturally relevant instruction has important implications. It has been the author's experience that special needs children begin to realize greater success when the remedial instruction is less skills-directed and more process-oriented using situations the children find meaningful. They learn that they are already problem solvers and in this light their individual approaches, experiences and understandings are validated.

Math with a message. Another excellent way to integrate anti-bias curriculum into mathematics is by using information about diversity as the content for learning and practicing mathematical skills. When studying graphing, for example, have children graph the churches listed in the phone book by denomination. With the help of a computer their data can easily be converted to a pie chart. Compare their chart with statistics on global religious affiliation. This information can easily be found in a current almanac. Discuss the data and how their own community is similar to or different from the global population. Many students may be surprised to find that Christians are not the largest religion in the world.

Art

Dr. Jane Rhoades-Hudak grew up in Appalachia among people for whom art was not just a subject or an activity, but also an expression of their mountain culture. Today considered collectibles, the wooden and metal artifacts they created primarily served a utilitarian purpose, yet were pleasing to behold. They were crafted of materials indigenous to the region using skills that had been handed down over generations.

An examination of any culture shows that the creation of art is an important aspect in helping to convey a sense of the people, their traditions and their values that words alone may fail to adequately describe. Although all cultures produce art, not all art is valued by mainstream society as being worthy of the same distinction or praise. The works may represent equally high degree of skill, but the culture(s) they represent may be viewed through a biased lens.

The ballet, the symphony and expensively framed oil portraits in major art museums all denote an air of high culture and good taste. Creators of such art were formally trained in a particular style that is reflective of a European history and people. To enjoy this art, one must often pay to view it and dress and behave in a manner that is considered "cultured and dignified." Politically powerful organizations use their political and social influence to promote their "art" and deny funds when the art deviates too far from what they consider to be socially acceptable and enriching. (The cultural battle around the National Endowment for the Arts is one example.)

On the other hand, art of the "people," often referred to as "folk art" or "arts and crafts," is often found close to where it was produced, is accessible for little or no cost, and requires no specific dress or manners to enjoy it. Wherever one travels in America, one can find art that reflects the local flair and culture(s). While this art is enjoyed by many, the formal art community often judges it to be less sophisticated or valuable.

In today's classrooms, children seldom learn of this bias toward certain styles of art and even more infrequently study ways to minimize its influence. It is unrealistic to expect everyone to like every painting, drawing or sculpture created, and this should not be the intent of the art teacher. It is reasonable, however, to teach children to base their opinions on the attributes of the art itself, rather than on its acceptance as "true" art. Students should learn to appreciate how each piece of art provides them a greater awareness of the artist and his or her culture.

Rhoades-Hudak (1995) recommends teachers in anti-bias classrooms use a series of specific questions to help children think more deeply about the cultural context of art and the existence of bias. A few such questions are:

- What emotions, values and/or qualities are being communicated?
- What does the artwork (techniques and materials used) tell us about the artist or his or her culture?
- Is the art "pleasing" or "not pleasing" and what are the reasons for such a consideration?

Whose art? How do we judge it? An art activity for older children uses a variety of examples of "formal" (pictures of European classics) art and folk art. Pictures of both formal and folk art are available in reference books, multimedia or on the World Wide Web. The teacher presents the students with a variety of artistic examples and applies the questions described by Rhodes-Hudak (1995) to promote a discussion. Students are encouraged to express their perceptions of each piece's "value." As students carefully consider the art, it becomes necessary to consider the artist and the cultural context in which it was developed, as well. Bias, which causes one to value the class or culture of one artist over another, is replaced as a deeper and more objective understanding of the role of art in culture develops. Teachers and their students may want to create their own "museums of art" that inclusively reflect the variety of art present in today's world.

Science, Technology and Society

Science, technology and society (STS) lessons differ from traditional science lessons because STS allows us to see how bias in science may be used to rationalize things people do and the decisions they make that benefit the interests of the majority often at the expense of the less powerful. Take plant growth, propagation and harvesting as a sample lesson. These processes cannot occur without some sort of effect on human beings and the environment. Teaching about plants (or any science topic) without discussing its context or impact does little to develop student scientists who can see beyond their own cultural and personal experiences.

In the plant growth lesson, STS would include an anti-bias focus that guides students to consider more deeply the implications of science. In examining how plants grow (or are grown) in many places today other than where they indigenously began, a teacher may lead students to question how this is done and why. When plants are farmed where they do not naturally occur, how must their requirements be met and at what cost? What is the impact on their new environment and its ecology? How is their propagation sustained? Because the new ecosystem of the farmed plant almost assuredly will be different from the one in which the plant originated, what artificial supports for survival are necessary and what are the consequences? If irrigation is required, from where will the water come and how does this affect people living nearby and the environment downstream? If chemicals, pesticides and fertilizers are used to sustain the orchard or farm, what will happen to the ground water as a result of runoff? How toxic are these chemicals to those who harvest the crop? Are the workers who harvest the crop paid a living wage?

Through such explorations, children often come to realize that products they take for granted may be acquired at great cost to other individuals. The individuals who pay the greatest cost are often people of color who are economically disadvantaged. As consumers, we may inadvertently support practices that perpetuate inequalities in society.

Birds of a feather. Diversity in nature is a topic that seems to intrigue students. The topic of "birds" is ideal for an integrated curriculum activity. Students should have access to a variety of resources they can use to investigate a range of birds and the characteristics particular to each. For instance, shore birds may have scooping bills to collect and filter plants and organisms living in the water. Birds of prey have talons for catching and holding their victims and sharp beaks for ripping and tearing meat. Discuss with students the characteristics that all birds have in common and some that are different.

As students grasp the concept of diversity in nature, this same concept can be used to discuss human beings. Read the book *People* by Peter Spier (1980) to the students. This book illustrates the variety of physical and cultural characteristics found in humans around the globe. After discussing the range of physical and cultural characteristics found among human beings, have each student draw or paint a picture of himself or herself. ("Multicultural" crayons or paints allow students to more clearly match the variety of shades and hues of human skin colors.) Pictures can be mounted on a bulletin board with a title such as "Human Beings: There Is Beauty in Diversity."

Language Arts

In language arts lessons, children learn about the power of words, which are often the vehicle used for sharing bias. Many thoughtful stories and poems (many of them listed in previous chapters of this book) can help children to explore a range of cultures, understand the damaging effects of bias and develop empathy for others.

Poems with a purpose. The following poem is an excellent tool for discussing how words develop social meaning. In the poem "Me" (*Salt Lake Tribune*, 1994) the author uses the term "colored" in an ironic way.

Me
When I was born - I was black
When I grew up - I was black
When I am sick - I am black
When I go out in the sun - I am black
When I am cold - I am black
When I die - I am black
But you . . .
When you were born - you were pink
When you grew up - you were white
When you are sick - you turn green
When you go out in the sun - you turn tan
When you are cold - you turn blue
When you die - you turn gray
And you have the nerve to call me "colored"?

After sharing this poem, ask students to research the historical meaning of the term "colored." Why is this term considered offensive to African Americans today? If a term is offensive to a group of people to whom it refers (e.g., colored, chick, Indian) what can and should we do?

Understanding and appreciating dialects. An area that naturally lends itself to anti-bias teaching is the study of dialects. Dialects abound in our classrooms as increasing numbers of minority students enter schools. A dialect is a variation of a language whose speakers can be identified as coming from a particular region or social group (Dandy, 1991). In our families at home, we may use a dialect entirely different from the one we learn at school. With our friends we may use slang and syntax not used in other contexts. When teachers address students or parents, they adopt the standard code—matching the demands of the situation with the grammar and vocabulary that is deemed appropriate. In schools, children seldom learn of their multilingual capabilities and, therefore, fail to comprehend the real power of language, which is not just to convey a message but also to share a culture.

Reactions to dialects vary. Southern and African American dialects, for example, both stem from similar linguistic roots. Yet those who speak them are perceived differently. Southern dialect spoken by whites is often thought of as genteel and charming, while African American English is typically perceived as ignorant or low class. It is not enough in an anti-bias classroom merely to note that differences exist, particularly when societal responses to these culturally based variations are not equal. Educators must guide their students to develop accurate knowledge and positive attitudes toward linguistic diversity.

Many children's books allow extensive study of cultural variation. A good example is *Flossie and the Fox* (Mikissack, 1986), a rural southern "Little Red Riding Hood" story written in African American rural dialect. In using a book such as this, a five-step procedure is suggested for exploring linguistic bias (Barta & Grindler, in press). Step one entails children reading or listening to the story. In step two, the teacher helps her or his students identify cultural aspects of character(s) and language that are different from those of the dominant culture. To explore bias and extend the learning, students could identify, list or chart ways in which the writer uses his or her dialect to express thoughts and feelings. Specific words or phrases could be listed and their meanings interpreted into "standard" English. Discussions of the ways that some individuals or society may perceive, evaluate and respond negatively to these linguistic differences will make up step three. During step four, students describe the literal message the speaker is trying to convey. When the intent of the speaker is analyzed, students realize they probably have communicated the same message. The difference this time is that a minority dialect is being used to best reflect the speaker's experience and perspective.

During the final step, students trace the history and development of the dialect. The culturally based vocabulary, grammar and syntax used to describe their experience and perspective typically follow sophisticated and systematic grammatical conventions. They usually find that the dialect, previously devalued, is as rule bound and grammatically systematic as the "standard" English they study. Children helped to this realization can marvel at the complexity and diversity of the multiple dialects of English.

Ugly adjectives. "Sticks and stones may break my bones but words will never hurt me" is a common children's chant. As children increase their vocabularies it is important that they learn how words can be used to either uplift and inspire or diminish and hurt. Often, children use words to describe others (sissy, ugly, retarded) without considering what effect those words may have on people.

Show students a list of adjectives that includes words such as "smart," "friendly," "compassionate" and "helpful," as well as "lazy," "dirty," "stupid," "dishonest" and "irresponsible." Have students read each adjective and discuss its meaning. Pass students three sticky labels and have them randomly select three words from the list and write each one on a label. Collect all labels, place them face down on a desktop and shuffle them around. Ask students to come and collect three labels without looking at what has been written on them. When students are seated, have them place their labels on the back of the nearest student (who has not yet been "labeled"). Give students time to circulate and read each other's labels. Next, with the help of a friend, students should remove their labels. Ask students to express how it felt to be labeled even when the act was entirely random. Help students to understand that negative labels can cause pain and that people's perceptions of themselves and others are influenced by the use of such labels. This activity can be extended by having students look for labels that are used in everyday life. A newspaper study of letters to the editor, particularly when controversial topics such as affirmative action or immigration quotas are being discussed, is a great place to start.

Wall of shame. Much of the prejudice and discrimination children learn is a result of experiencing the "status quo." Social attitudes and perspectives portrayed through television and radio can implicitly or explicitly teach bias to children. Seemingly innocuous phrases used in common language (such as "she took it like a man" or "he throws like a girl") misrepresent individual differences. Teachers can encourage students to vigilantly assess what they see or hear on television or read in newspapers and magazines for examples of media-perpetuated bias. When they hear a stereotype or see a biased image they can bring it in or describe it and then it can be added to a "Wall of Shame" collage. When students learn to identify bias they become more capable of confronting and eliminating it.

Social Studies

A major goal of social studies education is the development of citizens who can function successfully within a culturally diverse and democratic society (Martorella, 1994). Thus, anti-bias education is a central component of the social studies curriculum. Here are some sample activities.

Heroes and sheroes. Historically, notable women and minorities have been relatively absent from curriculum materials presented to children (Martorella, 1994). The effects of this curricular bias can be seen when children discuss their heroes and sheroes. To redress this, teachers need to point out the absence of information regarding the contributions and achievements of women and people of color. This activity will help students to recognize and discuss the significant social contributions made by diverse groups of women and men.

Ask students individually to list "heroes" and "sheroes" from each of these groups:
European American
Native American
Hispanic or Latino
Asian American
African American
People with Disabilities
Gay/Lesbian

Create a large master list from the names individual students contribute. As a group, discuss characteristics that contribute to someone being considered a "hero." (They usually say a hero/shero is one who has done something courageous for other people.) Analyze the list with your class. What conclusions can be made from the list? Are there biases or stereotypes evident in the names listed? What do the names on the list reveal about people we think of as heroes and sheroes. Review names to determine which people are current heroes and sheroes and which are historical. What are the people known for? Is there agreement about the names that are on the list? (Do entertainers and sports stars qualify as heroes? Are some of the people on the list personal heroes, but not famous heroes?) How can we account for the names that are on the list? How do people become known as heroes and sheroes?

Teachers may want to continue this discussion by having students research heroes and sheroes from categories that are underrepresented on the board. Some examples of diverse heroes and sheroes may include: Rosa Parks, Harriet Tubman, Amelia Earhart and Chief Joseph, to name only a few.

Where on earth. On the typical classroom world map, Europe is in the center. While all maps distort parts of the world in order to portray a spherical object as flat, the projections used in most classroom maps significantly distort (showing them larger than they actually are) the countries in the northern hemisphere. Greenland appears to be the size of South America, for example, when in reality it is about the size of Mexico. Some world maps may even bisect the continent of Asia and place half of it on one side of the map and half on the other. Although subtle, various map projections give messages to us that may distort our understanding and reinforce biased perceptions of our place in the world (e.g., countries where Caucasians live appear to be larger than they actually are).

Children can develop new insights into their perspectives of the earth and the global community. First, have students explore and describe their ethnic ancestry. Use a map of the world to place pins where their ancestors lived. Stories (real or imaginative) can be composed describing the journey of their ancestors to the United States. Teachers and students may also research how many cultural groups (Jews, Latinos, Japanese, Irish and Mormons, to name a few) encountered discrimination and prejudice after they migrated. Findings can then be related to the experiences of immigrants today.

Next, look at a traditional world map. Discuss how it is presented and briefly discuss how all maps distort the physical world. Teachers can provide older children with a copy of a world map that has no writing on it. Turn the map upside down and label the continents on it. (Antarctica would be at the top of the map.) Have children identify their ancestral country of origin and the place where they currently live. How do continents and specific countries look when viewed from this perspective? How does looking at the map from a different perspective change our view of our place in the world?

First thoughts. As students study people and society, they benefit from recognizing the stereotypes that they and others may hold about various groups of people. Stereotypes limit our thinking and always inaccurately portray some individuals because individual differences exist even within the same population.

Create a large chart with a variety of people (e.g., boys, girls, homeless people, people in wheelchairs, gay men and lesbians) listed at the top. Ask students to anonymously write on a paper strip the "first thought" that comes to mind when thinking of each type of person listed. For each category of people, sort the first thoughts into positive, negative or neutral piles. Attach the strips of papers to the chart. Ask your students to analyze the results. How many of the first thoughts were negative? How many were positive? Where did these first thoughts come from? Help students to understand that these first thoughts may be stereotypical and if we do not take care they can influence our interactions with individuals. Encourage students to monitor their first thoughts and recognize that actions should not be based on stereotypes, but rather on reasoned assessments of an individual person's behavior and interactions.

Banners and slogans. Students can apply art and/or computer-drawing skills within an anti-bias context when they design posters and T-shirt slogans promoting non-discriminatory and anti-prejudice messages. Several slogan ideas might be: "ERASISM," "ONE WORLD, ONE PEOPLE," "CELEBRATE DIVERSITY!" These banners and slogans can be used to kick off a series of preplanned activities in schools with a pledge to dedicate a week, a month or a year to decreasing prejudice and discrimination.

"Teacher, they called me a Qu___!" It seems society, in general, provides little support for boys and girls who enjoy games, clothing and activities typically "reserved" for the opposite sex. When a girl eschews dresses and can throw a ball, run as fast or climb trees as well as a boy, she is considered to be a "tomboy." Boys are called "sissies" if they cry, play with dolls or take ballet. As children grow older, terms like "tomboy" and "sissy" may be replaced with more damaging words like "queer," "fag," "homo" or "dyke." Children sometimes adopt these words to degrade peers who do not meet stereotyped notions of gender-appropriate dressing, thinking or behavior. These words are also used as powerful verbal weapons to

provoke, anger or hurt people who are gay or straight. Regardless of the context, such words carry a strong message to people of all ages that being gay or lesbian or not following strict gender scripts is something bad. An anti-bias curriculum teaches children to examine stereotypes and discriminatory actions, including those related to sexual orientation.

Just as a teacher would not allow students to use racist terms, the use of homophobic words requires an immediate teacher response. Children must learn that name calling of any kind is unacceptable. Byrnes (1995) describes several actions a teacher can take in response. First, teachers should discuss with students what instigated the name calling and what the student was really trying to communicate. (Many times children do not even understand what the terms mean, only that they are powerful and hurtful.) Students should be helped to understand that such name calling (because it is intended to deprecate someone) is hurtful not only to the individual to whom it was directed, but also to all individuals who are gay or lesbian and to all the friends and loved ones of such individuals. While a student may find a person's sexual orientation to be unacceptable (for religious reasons perhaps), it is not acceptable to engage in hateful and discriminatory actions against that person. Children should be given opportunities to think about and develop more appropriate ways to act and react when becoming angry or frustrated with someone.

Whose job is it? In a social studies unit on "community helpers," students could work cooperatively to cut out pictures of people from magazines and newspapers (select many sources; e.g., *Ebony, Ms., Newsweek*). Children then assign "jobs" to the people in the pictures. The jobs might include firefighter, police officer, nurse, doctor, teacher, cab driver, cleaning person, chef or president of a company. Make sure to stretch student's thinking by including job titles that traditionally have been considered gender or ability specific. Expose bias through discussion when the students are finished assigning their jobs. Tabulate the number of men and women doing the various jobs. Are people of color equally distributed across the occupations? Do students have a person in a wheelchair doing an important job, a woman as an executive or a man caring for children? After analyzing the data discuss the social implications of this activity. What do the students' findings suggest?

Music

In teaching music, as with other subjects, teachers must do more than present different music and styles. In the anti-bias classroom, society's response and reaction to music and the diverse people making the music must be examined. Children can be helped to understand that we tend to enjoy most the music that we have heard most frequently and that we connect to positive cultural experiences. Children's enjoyment of music can be used as a tool for teaching important anti-bias messages.

Different notes for different folks. Children can bring in examples of their favorite music (provided it is age appropriate and its lyrics are not derogatory toward other groups) and discussions can be lead about what they like and do not like in music. By modeling acceptance of a range of music styles, the teacher can help children to understand that differences in taste do not mean that one group or another is wrong in their preferences.

As children share their music, they can be helped to understand that as cultures have come in proximity to one another their musical traditions have often blended to create new forms of music. Much of today's popular music (e.g., rap, reggae, country) represent a combination of various cultural contributions. Encourage children to explore the cultural roots of the music they enjoy. Through such research, children can come to understand that by sharing and enjoying each other's cultural traditions we can create something new that may be greater than the sum of its parts.

Celebrating diversity. Bill Schmid (personal communication, December 28, 1995), music professor at Georgia Southern University, suggests jazz is a perfect example of what can occur when diversity is validated. He observes,

A jazz performance is like a multilayered conversation among the players, with everyone accepting what the soloist of the moment is saying, and then validating it by emphasizing, repeating, using it as a jumping-off point for further exploration of the song.

One anti-bias music activity that celebrates diversity models the importance of each note or instrument maintaining its own identity when accompanying others. Groups of instruments (e.g., stringed, percussion) represent how each instrument within the group shares similar, yet distinct, characteristics. A teacher with a collection of instruments can model for the students their particular sounds.

Multicultural harmony. Any instrument can be substituted for the guitar in this suggested activity. The students can be seated around the teacher who begins by explaining that he or she will be playing a song. The teacher plucks one and only one string, thus reproducing the sound repeatedly. Initially, the students will listen intently, but will soon tire of hearing the monotonous repetition and will look quizzically at the teacher. The teacher then asks the students if they are fond of the "music." Generally, students reply that it is not music because music has more varied sounds. A short discussion of how people are like instruments, each making a particular note or sound, can ensue. In a band, no one instrument is more important than another. At times, some may be played more loudly or more continuously than others. Change songs, however, and each instrument has a different role. Students can be asked to consider how interesting life would be if we were all the same and remark how wonderful it is that so many different people exist.

It's in the words. Music can bring us together in ways few other subject areas can. Songs such as "We Are the World" (by Lionel Richie and Michael Jackson), "One Light, One Sun" (by Raffi) and "In Harmony" (by Alan Menken and Howard Ashman) convey strong messages of peace and acceptance. When selecting music, consider incorporating songs that include strong anti-bias messages. As children learn these songs, discuss the messages conveyed by the lyrics. Having children share such songs with parents at school programs and meetings is also an excellent way to let parents know what the school values.

IMPLEMENTING ANTI-BIAS CURRICULUM: CASE REPORTS

All these activities demonstrate how anti-bias messages can be easily integrated into teaching mathematics, science, art, social studies, music and language arts. Once a teacher starts thinking about all the ways anti-bias concepts can be integrated into the curriculum, it is hard to stop. The following two case reports illustrate this point.

That's Diversity!

For the young students in Carol Ellis's preschool class at the Family Life Center located on the campus of Georgia Southern University in Statesboro, Georgia, the year-long theme of "diversity" helps them make sense of differences they see and experience in the world. Carol's main objective is to make children aware that diversity exists everywhere. Diversity is a common occurrence not only among human beings, but also among all things. She incorporates the concept of diversity into virtually every aspect of her curriculum (e.g., the environment, pets).

She proceeds by asking the students, "How would you like it if everyone looked like me? She notes that she has never had a single student reply in favor of such a world! She explains, "If everything were the same it would get pretty boring and that is why diversity is important!" Without diversity there would be only one flavor of ice cream or one kind of dog. "Diversity means different and that is good," she adds.

Children's literature plays a big role in helping to develop her diversity theme. She does not shy away from sensitive issues because she believes when handled appropriately, children can feel secure about sharing their insights or asking their questions. *The Cat Who Wore a Pot on Her Head* (Slepian, 1981), for example, is an excellent book to begin a discussion about people who have a disability. Carol makes use of persons in the community to teach children about the purposes of wheelchair ramps, hearing aids and signs printed in Braille.

Carol seizes opportunities to replace stereotypical and erroneous information with more accurate descriptions. When a book was shared that described all the heads of animal families as male, for example, she pointed out that lionesses catch most of the food for the pride and care for the young cubs.

By the spring of the academic year, Carol's students have had substantial experience with the theme of diversity. As she models her own wonder, excitement and respect, her students grow to perceive diversity just as positively.

Perhaps the most telling indication of the effect anti-bias education has on children is in the way that they respond to diversity. Jacob, one of her 4-year-old students was walking through a mall with his father when they both spotted a man with a mane of dreadlocks cascading from his head. Jacob stopped in his tracks and stared at the man and the man stared back. After a silence of some seconds, Jacob said to his father, "That's diversity!" and proceeded on his way.

Lightening the Load

Chris Bowen, a 1st-grade teacher at Mattie Lively Elementary School, also in Statesboro, Georgia, personifies many of the characteristics of an anti-bias educator. According to Chris, many of his children come to him already loaded down with "baggage." The baggage he refers to is the prejudice and discrimination that they and their families have experienced.

Chris's community is probably not that much different from many other places in the United States. What is different about Chris's situation is that he has dedicated himself to helping his students develop positive attitudes toward diversity and to confronting prejudice and discrimination. He wants his students to consider many points of view and to learn the reasons why people have certain perceptions. The following several scenarios shared by Chris (personal communication, October 21, 1995) typify how deeply rooted prejudice is and how clearly aware young children are of race.

During our study of community helpers, the class took a walking tour of the downtown area to view the various businesses located there. Since our class was traveling independently from the other classes participating, we took a special trip to see businesses operated by African Americans. I did not tell students of my agenda, but after going into several businesses, one black student said, "Hey, Mr. Bowen, blacks work here." I replied to the student, "Not only do blacks work here, black people own the businesses." The student simply returned, "Well, I'm going to do that!" (The field trip was a success, reported Chris.)

The second situation shared occurred during an activity that had students working together cooperatively. As the students were working on the class assignment, Chris overheard a conversation between a black girl and a white boy. The girl stated that her grandma cleans houses after she gets off work. The boy relied in eagerness, "Oh yeah, well my mom cleans houses and a big hospital." The girl innocently remarked, "I didn't know white people could clean."

The theme central to daily activities in "Mr. Bowen's room" is how we treat each other and why. Chris finds many "teachable moments." During Thanksgiving, students discuss sharing and community needs, the hardships faced by the Pilgrims and the openness of the natives who met and helped them. The students learn to understand the needs, cultures and perspectives of both parties. Stereotypes and misinformation about the natives who met and helped the pilgrims are countered with hands-on activities. To counter the "all Native Americans live in teepees" belief, for example, Chris and his students used the jungle gym on the playground to construct a life-size model of a house used by the native people who met the Pilgrims. The equipment (virtually a perfect dome) became the scaffold that was covered with brown sacks to resemble the bark used in making wigwams.

Chris once talked about the time his class spent examining the life of Dr. Martin Luther King. As Martin's life unfolded, the discussion turned to how some people are considered less because they are a certain color. Chris supported his African American students as they shared their feelings about being black in America. The white children were awestruck. They had never heard race talked about so openly before. According to Chris, it was a solemn and cathartic event.

In this classroom, students are never considered too young to discuss and learn about complex social issues. Rather, they are respected for their wisdom, which seems to surpass their youthful years. Racism, inequality and oppression may not be topics we find suggested for discussion in the core curriculum, yet many children live the effects of these social conditions daily. Mr. Bowen is the type of teacher who does not ignore the reality of his students' lives. He willingly and enthusiastically helps his students to question and challenge prejudice and discrimination.

Conclusion

Classroom teachers who consciously integrate anti-bias activities into their curriculum can provide their students multiple opportunities to deal with and overcome prejudice and discrimination. Math, music, language, science, art and social studies are all reflections of what people do. They are the vehicles for helping us learn more about ourselves and others. Teachers can and must continue to seek ways to make their classrooms places where all are welcome and can succeed. By doing so, we emphasize our common bonds and come to understand and appreciate our differences.

References

Barta, J. (1995). Reconnecting math and culture in the elementary classroom: Ethnomathematics. *Mathematics in Schools, 12*, 12-13.

Barta, J., & Grindler, M. (in press). Exploring bias using children's multicultural literature. *Reading Teacher*

Byrnes, D. A. (1995). *Teacher they called me a_____!": Confronting prejudice and discrimination in the classroom*. New York: Anti-Defamation League of B'Nai B'rith.

D'Ambrosio, U. (1987). Reflections of ethnomathematics. *International Study Group on Ethnomathematics Newsletter, 3*, 3-4.

Dandy, E. (1991). *Black communications: Breaking down the barriers*. Chicago: African American Images.

Derman-Sparks, L. (1991). *Anti-bias curriculum: Tools for empowering young children*. Washington, DC: National Association for the Education of Young Children.

Martorella, P. H. (1994). *Social studies for elementary school children: Developing young citizens*. New York: Merrill.

Masingila, J. (1992). *Mathematics practice and apprenticeship in carpet laying: Suggestions for mathematics education*. Unpublished doctoral dissertation, Indiana University, Bloomington.

Me. (1994, June 8). *The Salt Lake Tribune*. p. B1.

Mikissack, P. (1986). *Flossie and the fox*. New York: Dial Books for Young Readers.

Pappas, C., Kiefer, B., & Levstik, L. (1990). *An integrated language perspective in the elementary school: Theory into action*. White Plains, NY: Longman Publishing.

Phillips, C. (1988). Nurturing diversity for today's children and tomorrow's leaders. *Young Children, 43*(2), 42-47.

Rhoades-Hudak, J. (1995). Recognizing the importance of cultural diversity in an art program. In R. Ragans (Ed.), *Art talk: Teacher's wraparound edition* (pp. 14-15). Mission Hills, CA: Glencoe, Macmillian/McGraw-Hill.

Saxe, G. (1988). Candy selling and math learning. *Educational Researcher, 17*(6), 14-21.

Slepian, J. (1981). *The cat wore a pot on her head*. New York: Scholastic.

Spier, P. (1980). *People*. New York: Doubleday.

Chapter 8

Diversity in the Classroom: A Checklist

Karen Matsumoto-Grah

This checklist is designed to help teachers and other educators effectively identify and respond to diversity in the classroom. It focuses on various aspects of the classroom environment, including curriculum materials, teaching strategies and teacher/student behaviors.

Teaching Materials

_____ Are contributions and perspectives of women and cultures other than EuroAmericans integrated into textbooks and other curriculum materials?

_____ Are women, ethnic minorities and people of diverse socioeconomic classes and religions portrayed in a nonstereotypical manner?

_____ Do the resource materials include appropriate information about religion when religion is integral to the context of the subject?

_____ Do textbooks or curriculum materials focus on "famous people," usually those of privileged class status; or are the accomplishments and hard work of poor and working-class people given equal focus and respect?

_____ Do the resource materials include cultures represented by families in your school and community?

_____ Do English-language learners have access to resources in their native languages?

_____ Are teaching materials selected that allow all students to participate and feel challenged and successful?

Teacher As Role Model: Questions To Ask Yourself

_____ Am I knowledgeable about the religious, cultural, linguistic and socioeconomic backgrounds of my students and people in my community?

_____ In my own life, do I model respect for, and inclusion of, people who are different (religion, race, language, abilities, socioeconomic class)?

_____ Do students perceive me as sincerely interested in, and respectful of, contributions made by women and the many ethnic, religious, racial and socioeconomic groups that make up the country?

_____ Do I know where to find resources on diversity issues regarding race, ethnicity, religion, class, language, disability, gender and sexual orientation?

_____ Do I respectfully accommodate students with disabilities in my classroom?

_____ Do I recognize and acknowledge the value of languages other than standard English?

_____ Can I recognize and constructively address value conflicts based on race, religion or socioeconomic class?

Teacher/Student Interactions

_____ Am I careful not to prejudge a student's performance based on cultural differences, socioeconomic status or gender?

_____ Do I promote high self-esteem for all children in my classroom? Do I help each child to feel good about who he or she is?

_____ Do I encourage students to understand and respect the feelings of others who are different from them?

_____ Do my students see me as actively confronting instances of stereotyping, bias and discrimination when they occur?

_____ Given what I ask students to talk or write about, do I avoid placing value on spending money, or having money or major consumer products?

_____ Do I put myself in the place of the language minority student and ask, "How would I feel in this classroom?"

_____ Do I make an effort to learn some words in the home languages of my English-language learners?

_____ Am I conscious of the degree and type of attention I am giving to members of each gender in classroom interactions? Do I have an equitable system for calling on students?

_____ Do I use gender-neutral language?

_____ Do I teach about religion, rather than teaching religion or ignoring religion altogether? When teaching about religion, do I:

- place religion within an historical and cultural context?
- use opportunities to include religion in history, literature and music?
- avoid making qualitative comparisons among religions?
- avoid soliciting information about the religious affiliations or beliefs of my students?

Teaching Children To Be Proactive

_____ Do I teach children to identify instances of prejudice and discrimination?

_____ Do I help my students to develop proper responses to instances of prejudice and discrimination?

General Strategies

_____ Do I involve parents and other community members in helping children develop greater understanding of the benefits and challenges of living in a culturally diverse society?

_____ Do I inform parents of my multicultural, anti-bias curriculum?

_____ Do I support and encourage the hiring of minority teachers and staff?

_____ Do I build a secure and supportive atmosphere by creating a noncompetitive classroom environment?

_____ Do I use opportunities such as current events to discuss different cultures and religions?

_____ Do I provide students with opportunities to problem-solve issues of inclusiveness?

_____ Do I use activities that demonstrate how the privilege of groups of higher economic status is directly connected to the lack of privilege of lower socioeconomic status people?

_____ Do I have students examine and analyze the representation of class, race, gender, ability and language differences in media and their community?

_____ Do I recognize that tracking reinforces classism and is counterproductive to student learning at all ability levels?

_____ Do I utilize children's literature to help students understand and empathize with individuals who have experienced prejudice and discrimination and to discuss important social issues?

Contributors

JAMES J. BARTA
  Assistant Professor, Department of Elementary Education, Utah State University, Logan, Utah

DEBORAH A. BYRNES
  Professor, Department of Elementary Education, Utah State University, Logan, Utah

DIANA CORTEZ
  Bilingual Education Specialist, Utah State Office of Education, Salt Lake City, Utah

ELLEN DAVIDSON
  Instructor, Department of Education and Human Services, Simmons College, Boston, Massachusetts. Teaching Associate, Education Development Center, Newton, Massachusetts

GENEVA GAY
  Professor of Curriculum and Instruction, Associate, Center for Multicultural Education, University of Washington, Seattle, Washington.

CHARLES C. HAYNES
  Scholar in Residence, Freedom Forum First Amendment Center, Vanderbilt University, Nashville, Tennessee

GARY KIGER
  Department Head and Professor of Sociology, Department of Sociology, Social Work and Anthropology, Utah State University, Logan, Utah

KAREN MATSUMOTO-GRAH
  Educational Consultant, Friday Harbor, Washington

MARA SAPON-SHEVIN
  Professor, Teaching and Leadership Programs, Syracuse University, Syracuse, New York

NANCY SCHNIEDEWIND
  Professor, Humanistic Education Program, State University of New York, New Paltz, New York

BEVERLY HARDCASTLE STANFORD
  Professor, Graduate Education, Azusa Pacific University, Azusa, CA